THE LOWER EAST SIDE

A Guide to Its Jewish Past with
99 New Photographs

Text by
RONALD SANDERS

Photographs by
EDMUND V. GILLON, Jr.

DOVER PUBLICATIONS, INC.
NEW YORK

Frontispiece: Shoppers hunt for a bargain on Orchard Street.

Published in Canada by General Publishing Company, Ltd., 30 Lesmill Road, Don Mills, Toronto, Ontario.
Published in the United Kingdom by Constable and Company, Ltd.

The Lower East Side: A Guide to Its Jewish Past with 99 New Photographs is a new work, first published by Dover Publications, Inc., in 1979.

International Standard Book Number: 0-486-23871-7
Library of Congress Catalog Card Number: 78-73209

Manufactured in the United States of America
Dover Publications, Inc.
31 East 2nd Street
Mineola, N.Y. 11501

PREFACE

It is the author's intention to present in this book a series of impressions, through photographs and accompanying text, of the way the history of the Lower East Side, from its beginnings to the present, displays itself. Since all the photographs (aside from those in the Introduction) are contemporary, and since they are arranged in a fairly coherent geographical order, this book can also be used as a guide, held in the visitor's hand as he strolls through the neighborhood. For reasons explained in the Introduction, the book focuses on the area's rich Jewish associations, but the other ethnic groups that have established themselves in the Lower East Side in recent years are also in evidence on these pages.

A number of people must be thanked for their help in the preparation of this book. Beverly G. Sanders aided so inexhaustibly in the choosing of sites and the research that she came close to co-authorship status. Valuable advice also was provided by: Susan Bonhomme, Ralph DiBart, Hyman B. Grinstein, E. Y. Harburg, Jacob C. Rich, and Zvee Scooler. The staff of the Local History and Genealogy Room of the New York Public Library were most helpful. Hayward Cirker, president of Dover Publications, paid close attention to the book every step of the way, and was important in its evolution.

Built in 1863, No. 97 Orchard Street houses the Lower East Side Tenement Museum, chartered in 1988 "to promote tolerance and historical perspective through the presentation and interpretation of the variety of immigrant experiences on Manhattan's Lower East Side, a gateway to America." It is the first tenement to be listed on the National Register of Historic Places. With exhibition galleries at No. 90 Orchard Street and No. 66 Allen Street, the museum offers dramatic performances, exhibitions, workshops and lectures. Walking tours explore the area's rich multicultural heritage. Educational programs bring American immigrant history to students and organizations throughout the country. *(Photograph by Wangsheng Li.)*

CONTENTS

Map of the Lower East Side

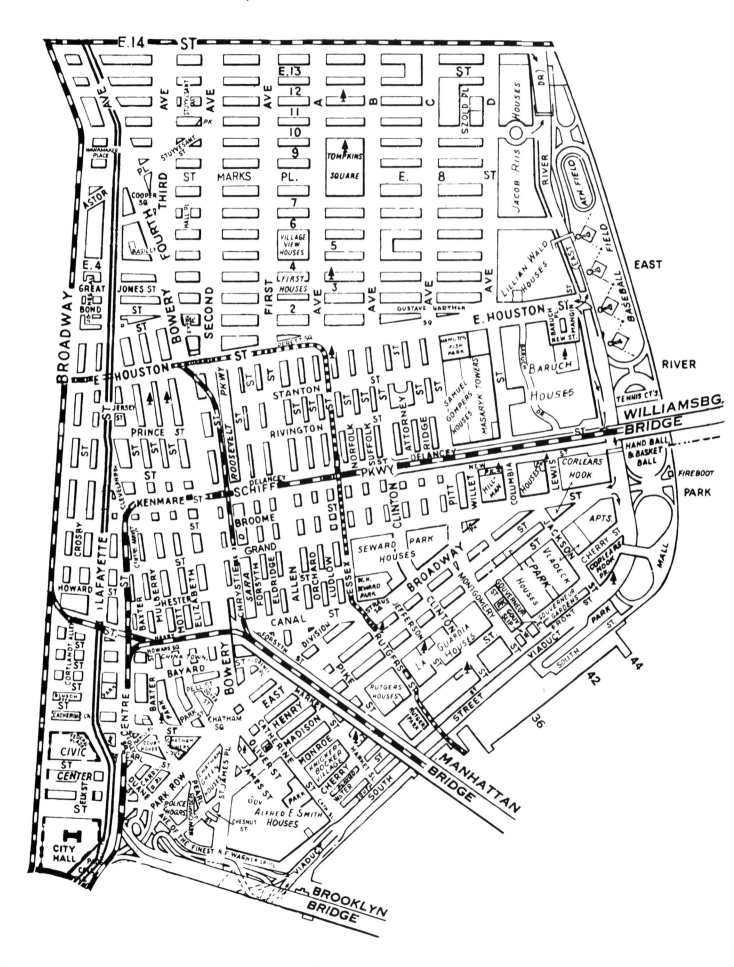

INTRODUCTION

New York is well known for its colorful ethnic enclaves such as Little Italy and Chinatown. Two of the most celebrated—the Black Harlem of today and the Jewish Lower East Side of just yesterday—are named both with reference to a geographical position and to ethnic composition. To mention Harlem is to talk of a bustling Black community that is centered around an area that was called Harlem at the beginning of the century. The fact is, the area and the population became synonymous, and as the Black population expanded, so did the area known as Harlem. Similarly, for a long time to speak of the "Lower East Side" was to speak of Jews (although the area was never exclusively Jewish, even when the Jewish community there was at its height). After all, Irish-Catholic Alfred E. Smith was as much a son of the Lower East Side, culturally and geographically, as Eddie Cantor was. Indeed, there was a time when the area was predominantly Irish. Today the considerably dwindled Jewish community is only one of a large number of ethnic groups on the Lower East Side of Manhattan.

Yet the fact remains that the history and character of the area have come to be defined in the American consciousness mainly in terms of its Jewish history and character. When, at the turn-of-the-century, such fine New York writers as Lincoln Steffens and Hutchins Hapgood wrote of "the Ghetto," they were taking in the Lower East Side and its Jews in a single term. For them, the two components were virtually interchangeable: the Jews and the Lower East Side were one. As a matter of fact, the geographical term "Lower East Side" is a somewhat evasive one if it is used without reference to the Jewish history of the area.

This was a shifting and expanding concept during a period of about half a century. As a term applying to a Jewish neighborhood, the "Lower East Side" originally (roughly, from 1885 to 1900) referred to just a few square blocks surrounding the intersection of Canal and Essex Streets with East Broadway. (Once called Rutgers Square, this intersection is now Nathan Straus Square.) After 1900, this concentration of Jewish immigrants from Eastern Europe and their children spread in several directions. One movement was southward and eastward, into the belt a few blocks wide that had originally separated the Jewish quarter from the East River. (The Irish population in that sector was never completely displaced by the Jewish influx.) The Jewish quarter also spread northward to Delancey and East Houston Streets. It was not until after the First World War that Second Avenue from Houston to 14th Streets became an important center of New York Jewish life and culture. Until then, it had little to do with the concept of "Lower East Side" for many. But, in terms of the Jewish history of the Lower East Side, Second Avenue is essential.

Today the ethnic character of these various sectors seems to represent an exact reversal of the chronology of their settlement by Jews earlier in the century. Second Avenue, the last of the principal areas to take on a predominantly Jewish character, is today the least Jewish of them. There the quest of Jewish sites is, as we shall see, more archaeological in character than it is in any of the other sectors. The next principal area, to the southeast, retains more of a Jewish character, at least along East Houston, Orchard and Rivington Streets, although this character is defined today almost entirely by commercial establishments rather than by residences.

It is not until you go south of Delancey Street into the original heartlands of the Jewish Lower

Three photographs of Hester Street published in E. Idell Zeisloft's *The New Metropolis* (1900) give some idea of the crowds that packed the Lower East Side, making it the world's most densely populated area during the period.

East Side that you can find a significant concentration of Jewish population, residing particularly in the large number of housing developments that have gone up all around that neighborhood since 1930. The continuing Jewish presence is evident everywhere—on the streets, in the stores and on the signs written in Hebrew or Yiddish that are posted on many walls. Here are a large number of New York's dealers in Jewish religious articles, as well as many of the city's foremost Hebrew and Yiddish bookstores and, eastward along East Broadway, an almost unbroken chain of yeshivas and rabbinical establishments.

As recently as the early 1970s, this area was still the center of what was perhaps the most important cultural institution of the Lower East Side, the Yiddish press. The chief monument to this institution, the ten-story building that housed *The Jewish Daily Forward*, still stands, towering above the buildings immediately surrounding it as it did above the whole area in the days when it was *the* skyscraper of the Lower East Side. Today the *Forward*, which is still issued six days a week, is in smaller quarters in another part of town. The old skyscraper is now the headquarters of a Chinese development group.

This is testimony to the continuing ethnic vitality of Lower Manhattan, as manifested by Chinese expansion eastward from Chinatown (and bringing in its wake, by the way, some signs of the presence of another Asian group, the Indians). Other parts of the Lower East Side south of Houston Street are Black and Hispanic. Northward, along First and Second Avenues, there are large concentrations of Italians and Ukrainians, as well as of other Slavic groups.

How then shall we define the Lower East Side for the purposes of this pictorial guide through many of the living sites of its history? Geographically, it is the area of Lower Manhattan that is bounded on the north by East 14th Street, on the south and east by the East River, and on the

west by a line formed by Third Avenue, The Bowery, and St. James Place down to the Brooklyn Bridge. Of all of these boundaries, the western one is the most tenuous, particularly south of The Bowery's terminus at Chatham Square, where Chinatown has overflowed it completely, penetrating to the very heart of the old Jewish quarter. So we must return at this point to the historical and ethnic part of our definition. What is special about this collection of streets is that it has formed one of the most celebrated settings for a unique kind of New York history—a Jewish one. Before we begin the actual survey, we should take a glance at the general and the Jewish history of the area.

It is significant to all the subsequent history of the Lower East Side that, whereas other neighborhoods just to the north of the original city on the southern tip of Manhattan tended to originate as suburbs for the well-to-do, this one was, northward from the Canal Street–East Broadway line, primarily for working-class and new immigrant groups almost from the outset. This was because the sector immediately to the northeast of City

Hall, standing between the city and what subsequently became the Lower East Side, turned into New York's worst slum shortly after it was developed in the first decades of the nineteenth century. The neighborhood occupying what is now Chatham Square was founded as a suburb for the well-to-do, but it was built on the site of the filled-in Collect Pond, and the streets and houses soon began to sag as the fill subsided. By the 1830s the rich had fled. Their houses came to be occupied by large numbers of the Irish immigrants who had been streaming into New York in pursuit of the job opportunities that had been created by the opening of the Erie Canal in 1825. Many of them worked on the docks of what had become a major port city, so their settlement tended to spread alongside the river on the southern boundary of the Lower East Side, after the well-to-do had left the area. This expanding neighborhood sought respectability, but the original Irish immigrant district around the intersection of today's Worth, Baxter and Park Streets, known throughout the nineteenth century as Five Points because of the five streets that then converged there, became a deteriorating repository for all those who had been left behind in the effort to "make it" in America. Jacob A. Riis, among other writers and journalists of the Progressive era, wrote at length of the crime and squalor of the Five Points district in his 1890 classic, *How the Other Half Lives*, as well as in other books.

The Irish famine of the 1840s brought a new spurt of Irish immigration into the Lower East Side, but by that time another significant group was making its way into the area. A large German migration to the United States had begun, particularly after the failure of the revolutions in Central Europe in 1848. In New York the new arrivals tended to cluster east of The Bowery from Grand Street northward, eventually reaching 14th Street. While Five Points formed a boundary that established Americans would not cross, to the adventurous immigrant it represented a kind of urban frontier. It was a criterion by which to measure his rise, and for the German immigrants in particular the rise was rapid. Unlike the Irish immigrants of that period, working people who sought their American opportunities in relatively humble occupations for the most part, the German arrivals tended to be middle-class in origin and aspiration — for these were the very people who had placed their hopes in the liberal revolutions of 1848 and had been disappointed. As a result, "Dutchtown" (based on the standard nineteenth-century American corruption of *Deutsch*, German, as "Dutch") took on a stolidly German middle-class character, with the cleanest streets and best-scrubbed exteriors in New York, and a somewhat more ornate urban architecture than Americans had hitherto gone in for. On a deeper level, the German community of New York was the first minority group in the city to have a fully developed high culture of its own, with a German-language theater and press, abundant public lecture programs and a distinctly European penchant for an intellectual approach to politics.

All of this reached a particular fruition after 1878, when another political disaster in Germany — this time Bismarck's antisocialist law — caused a new wave of immigrants with an intellectual bent. New York then became one of the world's centers of the exiled German social democracy; Karl Marx even thought for a time of making it the headquarters of the First International. The socialist *New Yorker Volks-Zeitung* came to rival the older, liberal *New Yorker Staats-Zeitung* for the role of the principal German newspaper of the city. Socialism became a prominent subject of discussion in the beer halls and cafes of the Lower East Side, as well as a main source of energy for both the English-speaking and German-speaking

circles of the New York labor movement. Ultimately, socialism also was an important source of energy for the Yiddish-speaking labor movement in its beginnings on the Lower East Side. In general, the culture of "Dutchtown" provided many of the patterns for the Jewish culture — with a closely related language — that succeeded it in the area.

Although there had been occasional, fleeting clusters of Jewish settlement in New York from the seventeenth century onward, there never was a fixed and distinct Jewish neighborhood in the city before the 1870s. This was primarily established by Jewish immigrants from Eastern Europe. In the colonial and early Federal periods, the Jewish population of New York and other American cities was primarily Sephardic, Jews of Spanish descent who had often spent a generation or so in an English-speaking country (Britain or the West Indies) before arriving here. Hardly distinguishable from any other middle-class group in the religious variety that made up the New York scene from the outset, they did not take to separate neighborhoods of their own. As German immigration rose steadily in the decades preceding the Civil War, the Jewish population of New York and of the United States in general became predominantly German. But though this development brought about a more richly autonomous American-Jewish life — creating the American-Jewish Reform movement, bringing trained rabbis to America for the first time, and establishing, in Cincinnati, the first rabbinical seminary in this country — German Jews in New York tended to make their homes within the general German community rather than as a separate Jewish group.

It was only in their commercial establishments that a distinct Jewish geographical pattern began emerging in the 1870s. The manufacture and sale of garments and textiles had already become something of a Jewish specialty in Central and Eastern Europe, and many of the German-Jewish immigrants had brought their skills in these fields to America with them. In that era Grand Street from Broadway to Essex was the principal shopping district of New York and its greatest department stores stood there. Since Canal Street, running parallel to Grand two blocks south, was the main location of the wholesale clothing and textile suppliers to these businesses, the area took on a high concentration of Jewish-owned enterprises. It was this situation, as growing numbers of Jewish immigrants arrived from Eastern Europe, that began to affect the residential patterns of the neighborhood.

Garment manufacture, from its earliest days right down to the beginning of the twentieth century, was primarily a cottage industry. Merchants and suppliers worked out of business establishments that were separate from their homes, but the people who cut and sewed the raw material usually worked in their own homes. In New York, this arrangement naturally encouraged those immigrants who were skilled tailors to live within a short walk of the places where they picked up and deposited the goods. The first distinct Jewish neighborhood in New York, then, arose in the 1870s with what might be called a tailors' migration from certain regions of Poland that were then either part of, or adjacent to, the German Empire, where the dialect spoken by the Jews tended to have a closer relationship to standard German than Yiddish often did. These Jewish immigrants from Suwalki and Great Poland, coming to New York specifically in search of economic opportunity, settled near the clothing establishments of the German-Jewish merchants, becoming, in a sense, an American Suwalki and Great Poland to the "German Empire" of the merchants. The first distinct neighborhood of these Polish Jews was at the corner of Bayard and Mott Streets, which was to become the heart of Chinatown in the ensuing decades. But soon they moved on and, seeking a place closer to the heart of the garment district, formed a cluster at the intersection of Canal Street, Essex Street and East Broadway. Into this neighborhood a sudden mass influx of Russian Jews began pouring in 1882.

Jewish immigration to the United States, like that of many another group, was always partly a flight from conditions made intolerable by poverty or by prejudice, and partly a search for the new opportunities that America seemed to hold out. But there have been moments when the balance of these elements has tipped sharply in one or the other of these two directions. The sudden arrival of large numbers of Russian Jews into the United States in 1882, which formed the spearhead of a mass migration that was to be as large and decisive as any population movement in history (including the original Exodus under Moses), originated as a flight from persecution. Having suffered for over two hundred years under conditions of poverty and oppression even more sustained and widespread than in most other eras of Jewish history, many of the Jews in the Russian Empire finally decided to leave after a series of terrible pogroms broke out in the Ukraine in the wake of the assassination of Tsar Alexander II in March, 1881. Suddenly, what poured out of Russia were not just clusters of migrants in search of better economic opportunities and living conditions, but despairing masses of refugees, most of them more firmly resolved in their desire to be out of

Russia at all costs than in any plans for the future. Many of them did not even have the means to emigrate, but in the first wave of response to this cataclysmic event, charitable organizations established by well-to-do Jews in Western Europe and America — including the *Hilfsverein der Deutschen Juden* in Germany, the *Alliance Israélite Universelle* in France and the Hebrew Emigrant Aid Society (later the Hebrew Immigrant Aid Society, or HIAS) in the United States — provided tickets of passage and wherewithal along the way. The vast majority of the refugees wanted to go to America, and since the European Jewish organizations usually wanted them to go there too, their transatlantic passage was made economically possible, though by no means easy.

For most of the new arrivals, the main route from the New York immigration reception center — Castle Garden on the Battery until 1892, then Ellis Island — into the mainstream of American life was through a job, often one for which the new arrival was solicited as he got off the boat. There were several such job routes into the Lower East Side for the Jewish immigrant, and foremost among these were the ones provided by the garment trades. But the immigrant garment workers of the 1880s and 1890s tended to have a wholly different character from those who had arrived from Suwalki and Great Poland in the 1870s. Whereas the earlier group had usually consisted of skilled tailors, coming to America in search of precisely this kind of work; now the typical garment worker was someone, completely unskilled in the field, who was simply taking the first job available. The industry had many low-paying jobs for the unskilled, and many immigrants were satisfied to settle for a job they regarded as merely a stopgap, one that did not require heavy manual labor (to which few Russian Jews were inclined in this epoch) and that was surrounded by a world of workers and employers who were all Jewish.

The situation in the garment trades in those years was marked by teeming activity and by transience. People who were mere workers one day might, for example, move a bit up the scale and become "sweaters" the next — small contractors presiding over several workers in their own tenement sweatshop. This is how the sweating-system worked. The small contractor, working with a margin of capital thin as a thread, would obtain raw material and an order for finished goods from one of the large merchants. He would then obtain the workers he needed for the assignment, very often in a public shape-up that took place each morning at the intersection of Hester and Ludlow Streets, where masses of workers and contractors gathered to bargain for jobs. This teeming intersection was dubbed the *Khazzer-Mark* (Yiddish

Opposite: Hester Street from Clinton, 1890. **Above:** Hester Street is packed with shoppers, 1898.

for "pig-market") by some unknown wit. The contractor then went with his handful of workers, who, in the early days, usually had to bring their own sewing machines, to his own apartment, often undersized and crowded enough for the family living there, and set up shop amid piles of cloth. This was the "sweatshop," one of which was described thus by Jacob Riis in *How the Other Half Lives*:

> Five men and a woman, two young girls, not fifteen, and a boy who says unasked that he is fifteen, and lies in saying it, are at the machines sewing knickerbockers, "knee-pants" in the Ludlow Street dialect. The floor is littered ankle-deep with half-sewn garments. In the alcove, on a couch of many dozens of "pants" ready for the finisher, a bare-legged baby with pinched face is asleep. A fence of piled-up clothing keeps him from rolling off on the floor. The faces, hands, and arms to the elbows of everyone in the room are black with the color of the cloth on which they are working.

If becoming a contractor was one way up, another way up and out was to take to the streets. One could rent a pushcart and fill it with all kinds of scraps overflowing from the wholesale stores of Canal Street — articles of clothing, buttons, bits of ribbon or cloth. Hester Street, just one block north of the wholesalers of Canal, and one block south of the retailers on Grand (from whom other surplus scraps could be obtained), became the great, teeming artery of the pushcarts. A few of the luckier street entrepreneurs might make it further up the scale out of the pushcart scene. One immediate step up, for example, was "customer peddling," going from door to door taking orders for secondhand clothing or buying clothing

Above: The scene on the corner of Willet Street, ca. 1900. **Center:** The ubiquitous pushcarts of the Lower East Side. **Opposite:** Ludlow Street.

with which to fill such orders. Eventually, one might accumulate enough capital to set up a store of one's own. There were always inspiring examples of these possibilities in view. Sender Jarmulowsky had started as a Hester Street peddler and became a banker, erecting, about 1895, the tallest building on the Lower East Side as a home for his establishment at the corner of Canal and Orchard (see page 70). And whatever happened, it was all intimately connected to the neighborhood; personal life and economic life were one.

Yet another way out of the sweatshop or its equivalent was an intellectual occupation. Some of the younger unmarried workers saved their pennies and went to school at night, eventually becoming doctors, dentists or lawyers. Others became journalist or labor activists — two very vital and well-manned occupations of the Jewish Lower East Side. Indeed, a special political energy came out of a situation in which young men and women of intellectual bent, bringing a socialist outlook with them from Europe, found themselves in proletarian occupations in New York. Whether they remained workers or not, their experience produced a working-class consciousness of unusual sensitivity, which was destined to play a prominent role in the American labor movement. Some of the most important institutions of

the Lower East Side came out of the labor and socialist movements, which were generated there under the tutelage of the German social democrats of New York.

It was the labor and socialist movements that gave rise to what was probably the most important of the Lower East Side's cultural institutions, the Yiddish press, which also got its start under German tutelage. It is no accident that *Forverts*, the name of what was in its day the foremost Yiddish newspaper not only of New York, but of the entire world, is not typically Yiddish, but is rather German-sounding. When it was founded in 1897, with a little help from the German socialists of New York among others, *The Jewish Daily Forward* (as it is called in English) named itself after the greatest socialist newspaper of the time, the Berlin *Vorwärts*.

Yiddish journalism in New York actually went as far back as 1870. Starting in 1885 there even had been a "daily" that came out three or four times a week. The *Tageblatt*, whose language in the earlier years had been more like a Judaeo-German written in Hebrew letters than a true Yiddish, was Orthodox in its religious outlook and conservative in its politics. Although it always had a following, eventually it was completely overshadowed by the socialist Yiddish press that got started in 1890. Producing a succession of competing journals through the early part of the decade, the socialist press began to bear its most successful fruit with the founding of the *Forward* in 1897. In the following years, other politically oriented Yiddish newspapers took their positions either to the left or to the right of the *Forward*. Sometimes they even took both sides at once, but all of them were bound to define themselves in one way or another with reference to this predominant journal. Following the route established by the *Forward*, for example, the principal Yiddish papers became not only forums for ideas, but also vehicles for popular, even sensational, journalism in the American manner, as well as for family features of a uniquely Jewish sort, such as the famous *A Bintl Brief* ("A Bundle of Letters"), a sentimental letters-to- and advice-from-the-editor feature that only in small part resembles the lonely hearts columns of the American press. In the midst of all this, the *Forward* and the other Yiddish papers also published, in their entirety in one issue or in serialized segments, the best products of Yiddish literature, providing sustenance and an outlet for such writers as Sholom Aleichem and Isaac Bashevis Singer.

There was only one other cultural institution on the Lower East Side that perhaps rivaled the Yiddish press in importance and vitality, and that certainly shared with it the quality of utterly characterizing its milieu. This was the Yiddish theater, which, though a worldwide institution like the Yiddish press, could also, like the Yiddish press, count its New York establishment as the most important one in the world. In the relatively secularized world of the Lower East Side, as compared with the old communities in Europe, the Yiddish theater and the Yiddish press provided the institutions for a new kind of religiosity: if the press was that world's Talmud, the theater was its synagogue. Sympathetic American intellectuals, such as Lincoln Steffens and the brothers Norman and Hutchins Hapgood, who knew German well enough to make out the Yiddish spoken by the actors, thought that the Yiddish theater was livelier and more interesting than Broadway, not only for what took place on stage but for the quality and passion of the audience response. Supporters of rival Yiddish playwrights or of rival artistic movements in the drama contended with one another in the theaters and cafes with the zeal of clashing religious sects.

Today, Second Avenue is best-remembered as the main center of Yiddish theater, but it did not attain this position until after the First World War. Earlier, Yiddish theater had been concentrated on The Bowery along the stretch a few blocks north and south of the Canal Street intersection — a district that no longer exists, owing to the widening of the approaches to the Manhattan Bridge. Yiddish theater traces its origins to the wine cellars of Jassy and Bucharest in Rumania in 1876, and then, for most of the following seven years, to Odessa in Russia. But the Tsar banned Yiddish theater from his realm in 1883, whereupon this lively folk art followed the mainstream of Jewish migration, and all of the principal companies replanted themselves in New York before the end of the decade. By 1890 one could see the outstanding Yiddish actors of the world in these few blocks on The Bowery: Sigmund Mogulesco and Boris Thomashevsky at the Rumanian Opera House; Jacob P. Adler at the Grand Theater. The fare ran the gamut from tragedy to musical comedy, from Biblical "opera" to modern naturalistic drama. Some of it was translated or adapted from the dramatic literature of other languages; much of it was written by original Yiddish dramatists of considerable power, such as Jacob Gordin, the author of *Mirele Efros* (originally entitled, rather aptly, *The Jewish Queen Lear*). All of it was acted in a characteristically broad "Russian" style, strong on sentimentality.

But to place special emphasis on these phenomena of secular culture is not to say that the traditional religious one had been left completely behind. There can be no doubt that there was a lessening of the power of religion in the transfer to American soil in the early years of the East European Jewish migration. Rabbis and traditionalists in Poland and Russia looked upon America as a land of heresy — the fact that German Reform Judaism was flourishing here was only proof of their point to them — and were extremely reluctant to come. In fact, not a single Orthodox rabbi from Eastern Europe reached American shores until 1888, and the experience of Rabbi Jacob Joseph in New York, powerless and ignored despite his title of Chief Rabbi, was enough to discourage others a while longer. But eventually they came, and though traditional religious institutions on the Lower East Side never were a match for the Yiddish theater and the Yiddish press in vitality and importance, they nevertheless became so firmly rooted that they alone among these institutions survive in the area today. In another generation, it is doubtful whether there will be either a Yiddish press or a Yiddish theater surviving in America at all, whereas Orthodox Judaism shows signs that it will be stronger than ever and the Lower East Side then, as now, will probably be one of its strongholds.

The life of Jews in America, like that of a number of other groups, has shown considerable geographical as well as social mobility over the years. With characteristic restlessness, many Jews who either were born on the Lower East Side or came there as immigrants have moved on. Large parts of the area have either wholly or partly lost their Jewish character, yielding place to other groups newly arrived in the city and seeking their way into the mainstream of American life. The

Jewish community, once dominant, is now but one group among many others. In either case, past or present, the Lower East Side has always been a preeminent locale for the colorful ethnic mix that is a part of New York's special character. Hutchins Hapgood, a descendant of seventeenth-century New Englanders and the author of the greatest single work on the Jewish Lower East Side in its heyday, *The Spirit of the Ghetto* (1902), wrote that he had a lifelong interest in "how individuals and groups who represent what might be called the underdog, when they are endowed with energy and life, exert pressure towards modification of our cast-iron habits and lay rich deposits of cultural enhancement, if we are able to take advantage of them." It was the Lower East Side that first brought Hapgood to this viewpoint and if the Jewish life he saw there was to a large extent changed and passed on to other locales, we may nevertheless perceive in the area today — both in its lingering memories and in its present character — the continuation of what he saw then. Hapgood saw what he saw by taking to the streets and observing carefully whatever struck his eye, and that is what we are about to do.

SECOND AVENUE
I: "THE JEWISH RIALTO"

For some people Second Avenue from 14th Street down to East Houston tends to define the old Jewish Lower East Side more than any other neighborhood, even though it was late to gain Jewish identification, because its heyday remains vivid in their memories. Others would exclude it entirely from the Lower East Side. But to do so would be to deny the Lower East Side a portion of its history.

Second Avenue, which flourished from the 1920s to the 1940s, was widely known as the "Jewish Rialto" because of its many theaters. The most celebrated was the Yiddish Art Theatre, later the 12th Street Cinema [1]*, at the southwest corner of 12th Street. Built as a home for the increasingly famous company that Maurice Schwartz had established at the Garden Theater in 1920 (see page 83), its doors were opened to the public on November 18, 1926 with an adaptation of *The Tenth Commandment*, by Abraham Goldfaden, founder of the Yiddish theater. In the ensuing quarter of a century, Schwartz achieved renown outside of the Yiddish-speaking world as well as within it, not only for his interpretations of outstanding figures in Jewish history and literature, but also for his Yiddish versions of characters from world drama such as Shylock. Other prominent theaters along the "Jewish Rialto" were the Orpheum [2], just south of St. Mark's Place, and the Public Theater, later renamed the Phyllis Anderson [3], at East 4th Street.

Another vital part of the life of the "Jewish Rialto" was in its cafes and restaurants. The most celebrated and important of these was the Cafe Royale — today occupied by a dry cleaning establishment [4] — at the southeast corner of 12th Street, directly across the avenue from the old

* The numbers in brackets refer to the illustrations.

Yiddish Art Theatre. Behind the cafe's doors, or, in the summer, in the outdoor section behind boxed hedges, sat writers, artists and intellectuals, arguing the merits of some new play, book or idea. Many actors also waited here to find work, for directors and producers not only came in person to cast their latest offerings, but also telephoned in when they were looking for certain performers. One Yiddish poet has written of the look of the place today that he sees in the suits and dresses hanging in the dry cleaner's window the ghosts of the men and women who used to hang out at the cafe. Another prominent spot was the Cafe Monopole, now a Ukrainian restaurant [5], on the corner of 10th Street.

As for the restaurants, they were for the grand occasions before or after the theater, rather than for everyday business, conversation or just sitting. Prominent were the "dairy" restaurants, such as Ratner's [6], in the space now occupied by the Dry Dock Savings Bank just south of 6th Street, and Rapoport's, another block south, which has also since moved away. In keeping with Jewish dietary laws, no meat is served in a "dairy" restaurant, but fish is, as well as vegetable dishes that are often ingeniously disguised to look and even taste like meat, such as vegetarian "chopped liver" or mushroom cutlets. But the most characteristic foods on the table were such celebrated dishes as cheese blintzes, or bowtie noodles with buckwheat groats (*kashe varnishkes*), or the huge piles of onion rolls that awaited you on the tables as you walked in. There were other kinds of restaurants as well: farther down the avenue, near East 3rd Street, was Moscowitz and Lupowitz, the Roumanian-Jewish Restaurant where one could eat in a murkily romantic East European atmosphere to the sound of gypsy violins.

1. The theater on the corner of 12th Street and Second Avenue was opened as the Yiddish Art Theatre in 1926. As the Phoenix it housed one of New York's liveliest companies in the 1950s.

All these establishments are gone, as, in some cases, are the structures that housed them. The National Theater, on the southwest corner of Houston Street, is now a parking lot. But the peculiar vitality they represented has often been passed down as a distinct legacy. The old Yiddish Art Theater, for example, has gone through several incarnations, some of them quite worthy of the building's splendid origins. In the 1950s it was the Phoenix, home of the liveliest theater company in New York at the time. Along with many revivals, the New York premier of Samuel Beckett's *Waiting for Godot* was done there in 1956, with Bert Lahr and E. G. Marshall in the leading roles. Later, as the Eden Theater, it did service for a while as a sort of nostalgic outlet for a burlesque revival by housing Anne Corio's *This Was Burlesque* and then the original New York run of *Oh! Calcutta!* In the early seventies its nostalgia came full circle and reverted to Yiddish as a company called Nostalgic Theatrical Productions, made up of outstanding veterans of the Yiddish theater, did one classic a year for several years in a row. In the mid-seventies, it served for a while as a movie revival house (shown here). This too closed, and at the present writing it is the Entermedia Theater, specializing in off-Broadway dance and dramatic productions.

Other theaters also have gone through difference transitions. The Orpheum did service for a time as a television studio. It was recently re-opened as a showcase for off-Broadway theatrical productions. The Public Theater (renamed the Phyllis Anderson) was doing Yiddish musical comedies into the early 1960s, providing a regular outlet for the talents of Sholom Secunda, composer of the Yiddish song made world-famous by the Andrews Sisters, "Bei Mir Bist Du Sheyn." Most recently it has been taken over by a Greenwich Village cabaret that features punk rock groups — which brings us to the more recent, and still current identity of this neighborhood as the "East Village." The "hippie" culture was at its height here in the late 1960s, and its main thoroughfare was St. Mark's Place, along the stretch extending one block in either direction from the Second Avenue corner. The lingering manifestations of the "hippie" movement — perhaps only awaiting a revival in some slightly updated form — can still be seen along St. Mark's, in the bookstores, clothing outlets, haircutting establishments and eating places that all bear a special stamp, and in the Theater 80 St. Mark's, near First Avenue, one of the liveliest movie repertory houses in New York. But the great symbol of the era is closed: the old Electric Circus [7], which became world-famous in the sixties as a center for rock music and the East Village "scene." Appropriate to the more traditional character of the neighborhood, this establishment had an ethnic origin, for before it became a rock cabaret it was Arlington Hall, a catering establishment that specialized in Jewish wedding receptions, and then it was the Dom, a Polish social center and restaurant where one could eat excellent sausages in a dark, sedate atmosphere. Just two-and-a-half blocks south of the former Electric Circus, on Second Avenue itself, is another onetime home of that rock music culture, also now closed. The converted movie theater just a few doors down from the old Ratner's was the Fillmore East [6], which subsequently did service as the Village East (whose sign is still visible) before it degenerated into a moldering wreck.

Although there are places on the avenue below St. Mark's place where the district, with some abandoned buildings, looks as if a bomb had struck it, there is nevertheless a continuing liveliness in the streets [8, 9] that defies pessimism. The Cafe Royale, with its sidewalk tables, no longer exists, but one cannot say there is no longer an outdoor social life on Second Avenue.

Above, left: 2. The Orpheum Theater, on Second Avenue south of St. Mark's Place, is one of the remnants of the days when the area was known as the "Jewish Rialto." **Above, right: 3.** The Phyllis Anderson Theatre, Second Avenue and East 4th Street, opened as the Public Theater. It continued presenting Yiddish plays and musicals into the 1960s. **Left: 4.** The most celebrated of the Second Avenue cafes was the Cafe Royale, at the southeast corner of East 12th Street. Its clientele included actors, artists and writers.

Above: 5. Another popular cafe was the Monopole, at the corner of Second Avenue and East 10th Street. Today the building houses a restaurant catering to the neighborhood's Ukrainian population.

Opposite, top: 6. For grand dining, residents and visitors on the Lower East Side patronized establishments such as Ratner's, 111 Second Avenue. The premises are now occupied by an Associated supermarket. The building in the center of the photograph, its front boarded up, was famous in the 1960s as the Fillmore East, a major showcase for rock music.

Opposite, bottom: 7. During the heyday of the Lower East Side, 23 St. Mark's Place operated as Arlington Hall, a catering establishment. Later it became a Polish social center and restaurant, but it achieved greatest fame during the 1960s as the Electric Circus, a mecca of the East Village "scene." Today, stripped of its canvas awning, it is closed.

SECOND AVENUE
II: BYWAYS OF THE PAST AND PRESENT

The Second Avenue neighborhood from 14th Street down to East Houston is more than an artery of entertainment. An interesting glimpse of the variety of its history can be had, for example, along the block from East 7th Street to Cooper Square. At No. 31 there is the Hebrew Actor's Union [10], still active, and living testimony to the day when Second Avenue was the center of Yiddish theater. But farther along the block we encounter signs of the other cultures of the area, past and present. At No. 15 is McSorley's Old Ale House [11], founded in 1854 and one of the few visible survivals of the era when the neighborhood had a large Irish population. Although McSorley's is still celebrated as one of the last of the old-fashioned New York saloons, with its bar rails, a pot-bellied stove and wooden floor covered with sawdust, it is no longer the impenetrable all-male sanctum of old, having been "integrated" by women in the early 1970s. There are also two establishments that offer testimony to the vitality of the Ukrainian community, the predominant ethnic group in the blocks immediately surrounding the intersection of Second Avenue and St. Mark's Place. The Surma Book and Music Company [12] at No. 11, is the largest outlet in New York for books and objects of Ukrainian origin and character. St. George's Ukrainian Catholic Church [13], across the street, has completed a brand-new home in the lot adjoining the old 1830s Greek Revival building (a former Methodist church) in which it had been housed for years. In the time since this picture was taken, the older structure has been demolished.

Opposite, top: 8. Youngsters on Second Avenue seek relief from the heat of the New York summer. **Opposite, bottom: 9.** An alfresco game of dominoes on Second Avenue.

The era of German dominance has also left its distinct marks in places. Among the most interesting of these are the two adjacent buildings at Nos. 135 and 137 Second Avenue, just north of St. Mark's Place, the Ottendorfer Branch of the New York Public Library and the Stuyvesant Polyclinic [14]. Both buildings were erected in 1884 through the charity of Mrs. Anna Ottendorfer, a wealthy member of the German-American community: one as a new home for the German Dispensary, which dated back to 1857; the other as a free library for the public before the city established its own public library system (and subsequently took this one over as a branch). Their facades reveal their German origin. On the Stuyvesant Polyclinic monumental sculptured heads of Galen, Hippocrates, Harvey, Linnaeus and other greats in the history of medicine are a flourish typical of the German urban architecture of the period. As for the library, the words *Freie Bibliothek u. Lesehalle* ("Free Library and Reading Room") are chiseled into the brownstone over the entrance.

The architecture of East 4th Street, especially on the block eastward to The Bowery, is quite redolent of the era when this was the heart of "Dutchtown" (Dutch being a corruption of *Deutsch*). Three buildings, Nos. 72 [15], 66 [16], and 62 [17], were public halls for meetings, concerts and lectures. No. 66, built in 1871, was the local headquarters of the *Turnverein* (Gymnastic Club), a German fraternal and gymnastic society. It also represents one of many instances in which the German community sponsored the beginnings of Yiddish culture in New York, for it was the site of the first performance of a Yiddish play in America, when an amateur group did a production of Abraham Goldfaden's *The Witch*, August

Above: 10. Down the block from "the Jewish Rialto," at 31 East 7th Street, is the Hebrew Actor's Union. **Opposite, top: 11.** McSorley's Old Ale House, 15 East 7th Street, is one of the last of the old-fashioned New York saloons. **Opposite, bottom: 12.** The Surma Book & Music Co., 11 East 7th Street, carries a wide variety of Ukrainian material. The building next to it, the First Ukrainian Assembly of God, was built in 1868 as the Metropolitan Savings Bank.

Above: 13. At the corner of East 7th Street and Hall Place (renamed Taras Shevchenko Place in 1978) stands the new St. George's Ukrainian Catholic Church. Its previous home, just to the left in the photograph, is a Greek Revival structure built in the 1860s. **Left: 14.** The Freie Bibliothek und Lesehalle (now the Ottendorfer Branch of the New York Public Library) and the German Dispensary (now the Stuyvesant Polyclinic), at 135 and 137 Second Avenue respectively, were built in 1884.

12, 1882. One member of that company was the sixteen-year-old Boris Thomashevsky, who later became the most celebrated Yiddish actor of his time. No. 62, built in 1889, is especially interesting for its outdoor spiral staircase partly covered by a semi-cylindrical screen, the architect's solution to the city's requirements for fire escapes. It is now the home of the New York Theater Ensemble. No. 72, a former concert hall, with its sculptured heads of great German composers above the second-story windows (Beethoven is on the right, Mozart on the left, and an idealized, periwigged Wagner, larger than the other two, is in the middle), is now the home of the La Mama Experimental Theater.

But beneath all these vestiges of immigrant communities, the foundations of the earliest American history can also be found along lower Second Avenue. Indeed, they form its most dramatic component. Certainly the most prominent and beautiful structure in the neighborhood is St. Mark's-in-the-Bouwerie [18], at the juncture of East 10th Street, Stuyvesant Street and Second Avenue. Begun in 1795 and consecrated in 1799, this stone Federal structure is one of the few buildings on Manhattan Island that survive from the eighteenth century. There are later additions: the tower was not built until 1807, the steeple was erected between 1829 and 1835, and the cast-iron portico was added in 1854. Today an active community center as well as a religious sanctuary, the church is known primarily for its association with Peter Stuyvesant, who lies buried there, and on whose farm (bouwerie in Dutch) the original chapel on this site had been built in 1660. In July 1978 a fire broke out in the steeple and quickly spread to the roof. Before the blaze was brought under control the entire roof had burned and much of the interior of the church was gutted. The old walls survived, however, and the community quickly set about plans to restore the church. Along Stuyvesant Street [19, 20], near the church, are some specimens of the era when it was still a private lane owned by the descendants of the last Governor of New Amsterdam. No. 21 [20] was the home of his great-granddaughter Elizabeth and her husband, Major Nicholas Fish, a hero of the Revolutionary War. Their son Hamilton Fish, eventually both a governor and a senator, as well as President Ulysses S. Grant's Secretary of State, was born here in 1808.

Further south, at East 2nd Street, are the two earliest nonsectarian cemeteries in New York. The New York Marble Cemetery [21], built in 1830–31, is on a walled-in plot of slightly under an acre at the interior of the block bound by East 2nd and 3rd Streets on the south and north, and by Second Avenue and The Bowery on the east and west. It does not come to the present building line at any point, and is scarcely noticeable behind the buildings and lots that surround it on every side. It can be entered only through the narrow alleyway pictured here, behind a gate that stands on Second Avenue itself. A distinctive feature of the cemetery is its lack of headstones: the buried are commemorated by tablets inlaid in the inner wall. More obvious is this cemetery's successor, The New York City Marble Cemetery [22] — note the addition of the word "City" to the name — built in 1831, and located on East 2nd Street, between First and Second Avenues. President James Monroe was first buried here, though his remains were subsequently removed to his native Virginia. Among the distinguished New Yorkers lying here are: two former mayors of the city, Stephen Allen and Isaac Varian; James Lenox, the founder of one of the collections with which the New York Public Library was formed; Moses Taylor, the prominent financier; John Ericsson, builder of the famous Civil War fighting vessel, the Monitor; and John Lloyd Stephens, the explorer of the ancient Mayan ruins of the Yucatan.

Tompkins Square, two blocks to the east, between East 7th and 10th Streets, is a most interesting sector. The buildings surrounding this fine sixteen-acre park and on the streets leading to it from Second Avenue [23, 24] were prominent among the examples of the middle-class solidity of "Dutchtown" during the latter part of the nineteenth century. The park itself was also something of a political hotbed, such as Union Square became in a later day. On January 13, 1874, for example, the German socialists of New York held a mass meeting of workers who had been left unemployed in the wake of the financial panic of the previous year. The police broke it up violently. No one was killed, but hundreds were badly injured, and the incident became known in the annals of the New York labor movement as the "Tompkins Square Massacre."

With this background of social consciousness, it is appropriate that one of the oldest and finest of the many historic settlement houses of the Lower East Side, Christodora House [25], should have had its home alongside the square, at the corner of East 9th Street and Avenue B. Founded in 1897 as the Young Women's Settlement by Christina MacCall and Sara Libby Carson, it was first located one block to the north. A year later, thanks to growing charitable support, it acquired a brownstone house at this location and took the name Christodora House to commemorate its Christian mission among the poor immigrant population. Its history is distinguished: the settlement was the scene, on March 21, 1914, of the first public concert given by George Gershwin, then fifteen years old, of his own works. The present sixteen-story structure, housing two swim-

Opposite: 15. Formerly a concert hall, 72 East 4th Street now houses the La Mama Experimental Theatre. **Above, left: 16.** The first American performance of a Yiddish play took place on August 12, 1882 at 66 East 4th Street, built in 1871 as a headquarters for a German gymnastic club. **Above, right: 17.** An unusual fire escape adorns 62 East 4th Street, built in 1889. **Left: 18.** Consecrated in 1799, St. Mark's-in-the-Bouwerie is one of the few surviving 18th-century buildings in Manhattan. It stands on the site of the chapel erected by Peter Stuyvesant.

ming pools, playing-courts and auditoriums, went up in the 1920s, when Christodora House was one of New York's great community centers and enjoyed abundant support. After the Second World War it fell upon hard times, and eventually reverted to the city, which used it for a number of years as a welfare facility. The building fell into complete disuse in the early 1970s, but it remains a solid and remarkable structure. At the present writing a neighborhood association is seeking to rehabilitate it as a housing facility for the elderly. The deterioration which has struck the east side of Tompkins Square is also evident in the abandonment of the East Side Hebrew Institute [26], another reminder of the day when this was the scene of a boundless optimism for Jewish immigrants, among many other groups.

Opposite, left: 19. Many of the elegant houses on Stuyvesant Street were built in the 1850s. Opposite, right: 20. No. 21 Stuyvesant Place is a charming Federal house, built in 1804 for Petrus Stuyvesant, the last Dutch governor's great grandson. Left: 21. Established in 1830, the New York Marble Cemetery stands at the interior of the block bounded by East 2nd and 3rd Streets, Second Avenue and the Bowery. Below: 22. Among the New Yorkers interred in the New York City Marble Cemetery, on East 2nd Street between First and Second Avenues, are James Lenox, John Ericsson and John Lloyd Stephens.

Left: 23. A scene near Tompkins Square. Below: 24. Tenements near Tompkins Square.

Left: 25. Christadora House, founded in 1897, was one of New York's great community centers. The 16-story structure on the corner of Avenue B and East 9th Street was built in the 1920s. **Below: 26.** On the east side of Tompkins Square is the abandoned East Side Hebrew Institute building, once one of the major institutions of the Jewish Lower East Side.

EAST HOUSTON, RIVINGTON AND ORCHARD STREETS

If you go down to East Houston Street by way of First or Second Avenue, you will be greeted by wide-open streets and intersections which do not seem typical of the Lower East Side. The fact is, they were created in relatively recent times. Allen Street, running from south to north and continuing uptown as First Avenue, was a narrower street until about 1930, when the thoroughfare was widened by the removal of the whole line of buildings and fronts on its east side. In 1942, the overhead Second Avenue elevated line was demolished, further opening the street. Chrystie Street, which runs northward into Second Avenue, was in effect widened a few years later when the short block separating it from Forsyth Street was razed for the entire length of the street and converted into a park, named in honor of Sara Delano Roosevelt, the former President's mother. East Houston Street was widened in the 1950s and 60s, so that the north side of that thoroughfare is formed mainly by the windowless backs or sides of buildings. The widening also created room for the bocce court [27] at the northwest corner of First Avenue and East Houston Street. Although bocce itself is a continuing reminder of the Italian presence on First Avenue, the inclusion of a growing number of Hispanics among the players and watchers shows another of the instances of ethnic succession on the Lower East Side. To round out the picture, in recognition of the Jewish history of the neighborhood, the broad intersection on which this takes place has in recent years been named Peretz Square after one of the greatest of Yiddish writers, Isaac Loeb Peretz.

The traditional Jewish presence shows itself most vividly when one goes south of Houston Street. From here down to Delancey Street there is a high concentration of commercial establishments of a distinctively Jewish character, especially on Orchard and Rivington Streets. The neighborhood is filled with shoppers from all over the city, especially on Sundays. As you walk along the south side of Houston Street, from the corner of Forsyth eastward to Ludlow Street, you will encounter a succession of food establishments, some of which have achieved national fame. All of them are good, but some are of particular interest. Yonah Shimmel's Knish Bakery [28], stands at the corner of Forsyth and Houston Streets. The knishes inside the unprepossessing little storefront are among the finest sold in New York and, therefore, in the world. The store was founded in 1910 by Yonah Shimmel himself. An old colored photograph of him in the window shows him as a bearded Jew in gaberdine and skullcap, but young, vigorous and looking very much like a man whose spiritual commitments did not interfere with his enjoyment of food. He was the *shammes*, or beadle, of the nearby Roumanian Synagogue (page 36), but that never was an adequate living for a man with a family, and so he opened this business that is now run by his grandson. Inside the store are tables where one may sit and eat, as well as a counter where one can order to take out, the knishes being constantly supplied from the kitchen below ground level. The classic knish is a baked mound of grated potato, mixed with flour, eggs and onion, but Yonah Shimmel's, like most New York kosher delicatessens, also offers one of *kashe* (buckwheat groats) instead of potato. Further-

Opposite, top: 27. Although bocce is traditionally an Italian game, a growing number of Hispanics enjoy using the bocce court at the northwest corner of Houston Street and First Avenue. **Opposite, bottom: 28.** Yonah Shimmel's Bakery, 137 East Houston Street, produces some of the finest knishes in New York.

more, unlike almost anywhere else, here you can get cheese, cherry and blueberry knishes, as well as other varieties. For a number of years, Yonah Shimmel's had a branch on Delancey Street, but that has closed, while the original establishment continues where it began.

Two and a half short blocks eastward, across Allen Street and halfway to Orchard, stands what many consider to be the finest specimen anywhere of that other classic of Jewish food purveying, the "appetizing store." Russ and Daughters [29], was founded in 1911 by Joel Russ and his wife Bella on nearby Orchard Street, and was moved shortly thereafter to its present location. The business got its present name because Russ had been blessed with two fine daughters but no sons, although now, since the death of the founders in the early 1960s, the store is managed by two sons-in-law as well as the daughters. A third generation also comes in to help out. On one side of the store, to the left as you enter, are the elements that go to make up the traditional New York Jewish Sunday brunch—several varieties of lox (smoked salmon), smoked fish of other kinds, herrings, pickles, olives, fresh cream cheese, and an array of salads: the aroma itself is where the "appetizing" begins. (The bagels and bialys indispensable to all this—bialys, short for Bialystoker rolls, baked with white pizza dough, are round like bagels but have a depression in the middle rather than a hole—can be bought at this counter only Friday afternoons and Saturdays, when Moishe's bakery, two doors away, is closed in observation of the Sabbath.) On the opposite side, to the right, are the dried fruits, nuts and candies that round out the essential offerings of the appetizing store. Overhead to the right is a portrait of Jacob Russ himself, looking down proudly on his human and commercial offspring.

Another block and a half to the east, at the Ludlow Street corner, is Katz's Delicatessen [30], one of the oldest and most famous of yet another type of Jewish food establishment typical of New York. Founded in 1898, the store and restaurant— also a family business continuing through the generations—remains to this day one of the finest purveyors of salami, pastrami, corned beef, and other "cold cuts" belonging to the realm of the New York kosher-style "deli." In the window are hanging salamis, and stacked bottles of Dr. Brown's sodas, a product that has all but ex-

clusively had its outlet in New York delicatessens for more than half a century.

The East Houston Street of good food and many visitors now begins to taper off as one continues eastward, but in that direction lie two sites of considerable historic interest. Both are old synagogues—the two oldest synagogue buildings in New York—standing in sectors that have otherwise completely lost their Jewish character and that are, in places, succumbing to urban decay. This is especially evident in the case of the first, the old Congregation Anshei Slonim [31–33] at No. 172 Norfolk Street, just a few steps south of Houston. This ruin, in danger of demolition, is the oldest synagogue building in the city. Built in 1849 by Anshei Chesed, the second German-Jewish Reform congregation to establish itself in New York, its architect was Alexander Saeltzer, the designer of the Astor Library (page 79), who was himself of German-Jewish origin. Temple Emanu-El, an older congregation of German Reform Jews organized in 1845, had recently established itself in a converted Methodist church on Chrystie Street. Although Anshei Chesed showed the boldness to erect a building of its own, its design adhered closely to the German ecclesiastical tradition. It is said that Saeltzer modeled this Gothic Revival structure after the Cathedral of Cologne. The towers originally were topped by two octagonal pyramids upon which stood ornate figures.

As "Dutchtown" yielded place to the growing East European Jewish settlement in this area, congregation Anshei Chesed moved uptown, eventually to merge with Temple Emanu-El. From 1874 onward, the building was occupied by a succession of Orthodox congregations. In 1921 it was purchased by a group of Jewish immigrants from the town of Slonim in White Russia (hence the name *Anshei Slonim* — "people of Slonim"). The congregation began to dwindle after the Second World War, but it held on until 1975, when it abandoned the building completely.

The story is different for the second synagogue, Congregation Chasam Sopher [34], No. 8 Clinton Street, again just a few steps south of Houston. That is to say, the story is different in its outcome, for its early history was rather similar to that of Anshei Slonim. The second-oldest synagogue building in New York, Chasam Sopher was also built by a congregation of German Reform Jews, Rodeph Shalom, in 1853. When Rodeph Shalom moved uptown in 1891 — eventually to find its present home on West 83rd Street near Central Park West — the old synagogue was purchased by a merged group of congregations from Poland that called itself *Chasam Sopher*, the "Seal of the Scribe." The name was in honor of a famous nineteenth-century German-Jewish scribe, Rabbi

Opposite, top: 29. In 1911 Joel Russ and his wife established their appetizing store, now located at 179 East Houston Street. The founders' two daughters and their families manage the stock of herrings, lox, pickles, salads, nuts and other Jewish delicacies. **Opposite, bottom: 30.** Katz's Delicatessen, 205 East Houston Street, is one of the oldest, finest and most famous delis in New York.

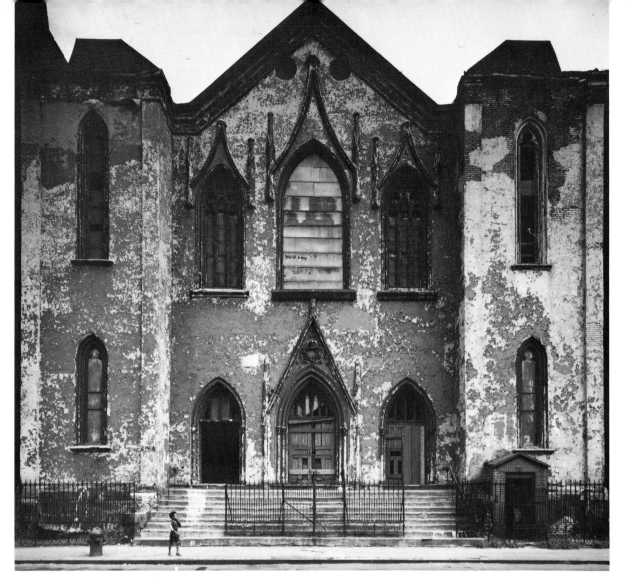

Above: 31. Built in 1849 at 172 Norfolk Street, the synagogue that housed Congregation Anshei Slonim is the oldest in the city. Today the abandoned building is in danger of demolition. **Right: 32.** The interior of Anshei Slonim. **Opposite: 33.** The interior of Anshei Slonim.

Moses Schreiber, who had dedicated himself to fighting the Reform movement in Judaism. This was a pointed choice of name by an Orthodox congregation that was taking over a house of worship from a Reform group, an act regarded by many Orthodox Jews in that day as being roughly equivalent to the cleansing of the Temple of Jerusalem by the Maccabees after they had retrieved it from Syrian occupation.

In the long run, the great struggle for this congregation, as for so many others on the Lower East Side, proved to be the worldly one of staying alive against the tides of social change and urban decay, rather than weathering religious factional strife. As with Anshei Slonim, the Chasam Sopher congregation has dwindled in the years since the Second World War. Nevertheless, it has held on. Many of the congregants are elderly, but even though they live a fairly good distance away — mainly in the East Broadway and Grand Street neighborhoods to the south — they have not lost their will to walk here to worship on the Sabbath. (During that period riding is forbidden to a pious Jew.) They also can no longer afford a regular rabbi. Nevertheless, their tenacity finally scored a victory, for when *The New York Times* carried an article on December 19, 1976, about the decay of this historic building, a flood of letters and checks began pouring in from all over the country, many from people who had attended the synagogue years before. A rededication was held in the handsomely restored structure only a few months later.

Going two blocks south to Rivington Street and then turning right, we enter another sector that, amid the seething change around it, has retained some of the character of an earlier time. At the corner of Suffolk Street is the factory in which Streit's [35], one of the leading matzoh bakers in the world, manufactures its wares. From the street, you can look through the factory window and see the flat, yellow, unleavened bread, flecked with brown, coming off rollers in large, consolidated sheets which are broken off by the workers and cut down into the smaller sheets that are packed in boxes for the market. Among the workers, you can as readily hear Spanish as any other language, and the "No Smoking" sign at the factory entrance is accompanied by an emphatic "No Se Fume" — both facts reflecting what is now the predominant ethnic character of the surrounding streets. Two blocks farther west, at No. 124 Rivington Street, near the corner of Essex Street, is Schapiro's Wine Company [36], the manufacturer of sacerdotal wine, another kosher product vital for Jewish rituals and, like matzoh, primarily associated with the Passover table. But this establishment, founded in 1899, also has entered the modern business world and can boast that their product is not for "special occasions"

alone. Schapiro's, which takes its visitors on regular tours of the premises, wants its wines to be drunk by all. It has added new flavors, such as honey wine, to the traditional list that includes Malaga, Tokay and Concord grape, and has extended its range from the old sweet wines to the more cosmopolitan dry.

Rivington Street becomes most lively as it crosses Essex Street, into which it seems to spill over with establishments extending in both directions. Bernstein's kosher Chinese restaurant (a true New York synthesis of ethnic cuisines) is to the north; the covered malls of the Essex Street Retail Market lie to the south. Just before Orchard Street, on the south side of Rivington at No. 89, is one of the most interesting synagogues of the Lower East Side, still pulsating with life: Shaarey Shomoyim, The First Roumanian-American Congregation [37]. Built in the Romanesque Revival style as a Methodist church in 1888, the building was purchased by the Roumanian congregation Shaarey Shomoyim ("Gates of Heaven") about two years later. With a seating capacity of almost two thousand, it is one of the largest synagogues in Manhattan. The congregation ceased to be primarily Roumanian many years ago and is today made up largely of the Jewish merchants of the area. It has long been famous for its cantorial singing, which may represent a partly Roumanian legacy, for although great cantorial singing is primarily associated in the Old World with Lithuania, it is well known that Roumania was the principal homeland, among Jews, of the passion for a good show.

Some of the twentieth century's greatest cantors (*chazonim*, in Hebrew; *chazan* in the singular) such as Yossele Rosenblatt and Moishe Koussevitsky, began their American careers in this synagogue. It was also the home of the greatest of all popularizers of cantorial singing, Moishe Oysher, who, from the 1930s to the 1950s, enjoyed a career in movies, radio and television as well as on the stage. One of Oysher's films, made in Yiddish in the thirties, was the story of a great cantor from a humble Lithuanian *shtetl*, or village, who went off to Warsaw and, almost inevitably, became one of the world's greatest opera singers. The synagogue was twice the starting point for such a story in real life, for both Jan Peerce and his brother-in-law Richard Tucker were cantors there before they went off to become famous in the world of opera. As proof of its continuing vitality, Shaarey Shomoyim is one of the few synagogues on the Lower East Side to have its own Talmud Torah, or religious elementary school.

Opposite: 34. Congregation Chasam Sopher has met in this 1853 synagogue since 1891. Although the congregation has dwindled and can no longer afford a rabbi, it has managed to continue its activities.

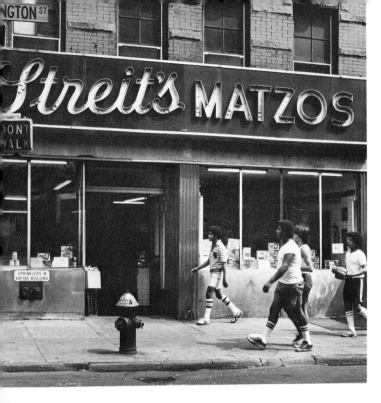

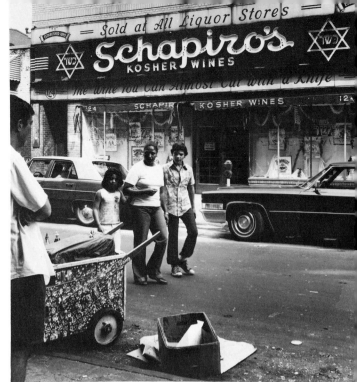

Above, left: 35. Matzoh (flat, yellow unleavened bread used by Jews during Passover) is produced at Streit's, at the corner of Rivington and Suffolk Street. **Above, right: 36.** Schapiro's, 124 Rivington Street, produces both table and sacerdotal wines. **Left: 37.** Famed singers Jan Peerce and Richard Tucker served as cantors at Shaarey Shomoyim, 89 Rivington Street, before going on to the world of opera.

Most of the Talmud Torahs in the area are minuscule independent institutions, usually located in a rabbi's study.

Crossing Orchard Street, we continue westward to the corner of Eldridge and Rivington Streets, where the University Settlement [38] stands. The example of Toynbee Hall in London, a gathering of a group of educated, socially conscious members of the middle classes within the slums of the East End, had begun to inspire American equivalents in the 1880s, most of them in the Lower East Side. The University Settlement Society was first founded under the name of the Neighborhood Guild by Dr. Stanton Coit of the Ethical Culture Society, in 1886. It changed its name in 1891, when it was reorganized under the presidency of Seth Low, president of Columbia University, and took into its ranks a number of the university's students and graduates. As a guidebook of the time puts it, the University Settlement Society, which had located itself at first on Delancey Street, was founded "for the purpose of bringing men of education into closer relations with the laboring classes of the city, for mutual instruction and benefit. It aims to establish 'settlements' in the tenement-house districts, where college men interested in the workers may live, and mingle with their poor neighbors, on terms of perfect equality." In this way, the eager young men could "carry out, or induce others to carry out, all the reforms, domestic, industrial, educational, provident, or recreative, which the social ideal demands." The University Settlement established itself in the present building in 1898. There was a women's equivalent to this in the College Settlement on Rivington Street near Orchard, founded by Smith College graduates in 1889. Although there are slightly older settlement house buildings on the Lower East Side, the University Settlement is the oldest such association to be continuously located in the area.

On the bustling stretch of Orchard Street [39–42], from Houston down to Delancey, we have reached the artery that epitomizes the Lower East Side today for many visitors. In a sense, it is the direct offspring of Hester Street (page 52), the old center of the world of pushcart merchandising that had typified the New York "ghetto" to outsiders at the turn of the century. Orchard Street was also an artery for pushcarts, until they were banned by the time of the Second World War. By then, the nature of streetside retailing on the Lower East Side had begun to change as the pushcart peddler was replaced by the more prosperous owners of storefronts, who set up stalls outside their front doors. Orchard became the main marketplace after much of Hester Street disappeared when housing projects were built in the 1930s, but activity overflows into adjoining side

38. The University Settlement, 184 Eldridge Street, was founded as the Neighborhood Guild in 1886, and was patterned after London's Toynbee Hall.

streets. The rushing flow of infinite quantities of small goods, and the spirit of bargaining that has always dominated it all — sometimes more in spirit than in practice — seem to cry out for the continuation of the old European tradition of the open marketplace.

The traditional intonations along Orchard Street — Yiddish and a Yiddish-accented English — are now rivaled by Spanish and by a touch of Hebrew coming from the Israeli merchants, the most recent Jewish immigrants. The items sold in this continuous and busy succession of stalls and stores still tend to be small and low-priced. Though there are abundant quantities of what is known in American-Yiddish as "shlock" (garbage), the astute shopper can also find the highest quality goods here at prices lower than those at which they are sold in chic uptown stores. The main emphasis remains on clothing — the eye is stimulated in every direction by a forest of pants, shoes, belts, ties, socks, shirts and dresses, some lying on the stalls, some hanging in the air. But other types of small articles — some say almost anything — also can be found here. Sunday on Orchard Street, when it springs back to life after the Sabbath closing of most of the Jewish establishments, has become a major New York institution, drawing visitors in such numbers that a recent law has closed the street to vehicular traffic on Sunday.

This page and opposite: 39–42. Scenes on Orchard Street. The merchandise displayed in cardboard boxes is characteristic.

DELANCEY,
GRAND AND ESSEX STREETS

Delancey Street was once a major Jewish thoroughfare for two boroughs, and its link with Brooklyn remains its dominant landmark. The Williamsburg Bridge [43–45] was the second steel suspension bridge built over the East River, opening in 1903, twenty years after the Brooklyn Bridge. It immediately encouraged the spread of Jewish settlement to new neighborhoods in Brooklyn, particularly to Williamsburg, at the other end of the bridge. Whether rabbis agreed or not, many pious Jews thought the bridge's length was a permissible distance to walk for visits on the Sabbath when its pedestrian ramp became a major promenade. Much of the area surrounding the bridge's entrance was cleared and Delancey Street, already a broad avenue, was widened for several blocks. Nevertheless, touches of an older New York have survived in its shadow, such as the row of Federal-style houses on Pitt Street [45], built in the 1830s and 1840s as the homes of well-to-do suburbanites.

Delancey Street itself is in transition, its older Jewish character still visible in many places such as Ratner's Dairy Restaurant [46], No. 138, but giving way in others to newer ethnic manifestations, particularly Hispanic. The old Loew's Delancey [47], a few doors from Ratner's, has been closed and been replaced by stores, but when this picture was taken in 1977, the splendid old marquee, a fine example of the movie-house Art Deco of the 1920s, was still in place. Movies were a particular passion on the Lower East Side, which supplied Hollywood with a lion's share of producers, directors, actors, screenwriters and other participants in the film-making process. The area once boasted many movie houses, such as the Apollo, Clinton, Ruby, Windsor, Palestine and Florence—all gone now. Another on this street, the Delancey, did service for a number of years as a Spanish cinema before closing recently.

An interesting example of the succession of institutions on Delancey Street is the recently vacated home of the Hebrew Publishing Company [48], No. 79, at the corner of Allen Street. This imposing structure was for many years the Bank of the United States. Largely Jewish-owned, it prospered for a long time on the Lower East Side, in part because many of the immigrants thought its name indicated that it was an official institution of the United States Government. After the crash of 1929 it fell upon hard times, and when a number of major banks failed to grant it short-term credit, many residents of the area considered anti-Semitism to be the reason. The bank finally collapsed in 1932, but most of the depositors were able to recoup a large part of their losses. Shortly after that, the building was taken over by one of the most distinguished institutions of the Lower East Side, the Hebrew Publishing Company, which has put out a wide range of books — religious and secular — in Hebrew, Yiddish and English. The company became one of the world's foremost propagandists of Yiddish literature when, shortly after its founding in 1891, it published Alexander Harkavy's *Yiddish-English Dictionary*, the first and for many years the only book of its kind. In 1976 the Hebrew Publishing Company moved to smaller quarters on Grand Street near Allen, just a few blocks south, and at this writing the old Bank of the United States structure still awaits a new occupant. The building did not originally stand on a corner, by the way. It was not meant to, and the

Opposite: 43. The Williamsburg Bridge links the Lower East Side to Brooklyn. Its opening in 1903 helped the Jewish community to spread across the East River.

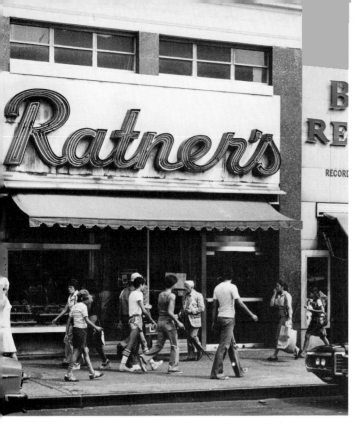

Opposite, top: 44. One of the massive pylons of the Williamsburg Bridge, designed by Leffert L. Buck. **Opposite, bottom: 45.** A few Federal houses, built in the 1830s and 1840s, survive on Pitt Street, in the shadow of the Williamsburg Bridge. **Above, top: 46.** Ratner's, 138 Delancey Street, is one of New York's most famous "dairy" restaurants. No meat dishes are served there. **Above, bottom: 47.** Loew's Delancey, shortly before the old movie house was converted into stores. The Lower East Side once boasted many movie houses; few are left.

unprepossessing view one has of it on the Allen Street side was the result of the street's widening in 1930.

On the corner of Forsyth Street is the former Forsyth Street Synagogue [49], another dramatic illustration of the cultural transformation of Delancey Street. Home of Congregation Anshei Ileya for many years, it now houses a Spanish congregation, the Union Square Seventh Day Adventist Church. The origin of the building remains visible in the round window over the entrance displaying a Star of David. A striking feature of this eclectic structure are the store-fronts on the street level. The architects provided them in their design to help support the synagogue. This interesting urban idea goes as far back as Cooper Union in the 1850s, which also had store fronts.

If we go two blocks south along Forsyth we enter Grand Street, one of New York's main shopping streets during a good part of the nineteenth century. To the right, a few blocks to the west, at the corner of Grand and Broadway, stood what was the main branch of Lord and Taylor for a number of years until 1871, when the store established new main quarters at Broadway and 20th Street. An important branch also stood at the corner of Grand and Chrystie. (Neither of the Lord and Taylor buildings of Grand Street are standing today.) Eastward, at the southeast corner of Grand and Allen, we can see what remains of Ridley's [50]. One of the great department stores of Grand Street's heyday, it originated as a small shop on this site in 1849. By the 1880s it had expanded to become the country's largest retail store. The building covered an entire square block, and was larger then than it is today (the Allen Street side was shaved down when the street was widened). Ridley's closed in 1901, a year before Lord and Taylor closed its downtown branches. The decline of Grand Street was furthered in 1903, when the opening of the Williamsburg Bridge put an end to the Grand Street ferry, which had attracted crowds of shoppers from Brooklyn.

Yet the street remains an important center for dry-goods establishments, and the recent move of the Hebrew Publishing Company to No. 316 Grand Street, just across the street from the former Ridley's, testifies to a well-warranted optimism about its future. Covering the entire square block that is bounded by Grand, Ludlow, Essex and Broome Streets, stands one of the foremost organs of the life of the Lower East Side, Seward Park High School [51]. Built in 1929 on the site of the old Ludlow Street jail, the school, named after the park a few blocks south on Essex Street (page 53), was until quite recently the only public high school in Manhattan south of Houston Street. It has served not only the Lower East Side (the actors Zero Mostel and Walter Matthau are

Above, left: 48. For many years housing the Bank of the United States, the building at 79 Delancey Street served as the headquarters of the Hebrew Publishing Company from 1932 until recently. **Above, right: 49.** As one ethnic group disappears from the Lower East Side, another recycles its buildings. Once the home of Congregation Anshei Ileya, the building at 126 Forsyth Street now houses a Spanish Adventist congregation. **Left: 50.** Subdivided into several stores, the building at the corner of Grand and Allen Streets once was Ridley's, the country's largest retail store in the 1880s. **Opposite, top: 51.** Among the sons of the Lower East Side who have graduated from Seward Park High School, 350 Grand Street, are actors Zero Mostel and Walter Matthau. **Opposite, bottom: 52.** The Beth Hamidrash Hagodol Synagogue, 60 Norfolk Street, was originally built as a Baptist Church in 1852. Designated a city landmark in 1977, it has been repainted and repaired.

among the more celebrated sons it has graduated) but also other areas of distinct character in Lower Manhattan, such as Chinatown. To this day, Seward Park can boast, among the rich ethnic variety of its student body (perhaps the most ethnically varied in the city), the largest number of Chinese students of any public high school in New York. Chinese is among the languages offered here for study, as well as Russian and Hebrew, reflecting two other ethnic components of the population it serves.

Continuing along Grand Street across Essex to Norfolk, we can see at No. 60 Norfolk Street, just to the north, the Beth Hamidrash Hagodol Synagogue [52], another heartening example of synagogue restoration. Built in 1852 as the Norfolk Street Baptist Church, the Gothic Revival structure was purchased in 1885 by the Orthodox congregation that is still housed in it. It is therefore the home of the oldest Orthodox congregation continuously housed in a single location in New York. In 1899, Rabbi Jacob Joseph from Vilna (page 10), was given the charge of this congregation with the title of "Chief Rabbi." It is now presided over by Rabbi Ephraim Oshry, a native of Lithuania and a survivor of the Holocaust. The building, a designated New York City landmark, was repainted and repaired in 1977.

Opposite: 53. Erected in 1832, the Church of St. Mary is the oldest Catholic church structure in New York. **Above: 54.** The stretch of Essex Street between Grand Street and Straus Square is one of the busiest commercial sectors in the Lower East Side. **Right: 55.** Determined shoppers on Essex Street.

Three and a half blocks farther eastward along Grand, at the "corner" of a part of Ridge Street that no longer exists save as a pedestrian walk, stands a proud continuing manifestation of the old Irish component of the Lower East Side. The Church of St. Mary [53] is the oldest Catholic church structure in New York, having been erected here in 1832 by a parish founded six years earlier. The brick facade, with its wooden trims and door-frames, and the twin towers, are additions dating from the 1880s, but the main part of the building, made of rough-hewn stones, clearly reveals an architectural style of the 1830s. Surrounded by housing developments, this church continues to serve the primarily Hispanic population that has settled in its environs in recent years.

On the section of Essex Street stretching southward from Grand Street to Straus Square [54–58], we are again in one of the liveliest commercial sectors on the Lower East Side, into which the Sunday crowd on Orchard Street often spills over. This is the original nucleus of the entire Jewish settlement of the area, and the solidly Jewish character of the sector still shows clearly, es-

Above, left: 56. A scene on Essex Street. The man in the center of the photograph wears the clothing, beard and long sidelocks that distinguish him as a Chassid. **Above, right: 57.** Essex Street probably has the city's largest concentration of shops selling Jewish religious articles and books. **Left: 58.** Lou the Pickleman vends his wares at 27 Essex Street. **Opposite, top: 59.** A scene on Hester Street. **Opposite, bottom: 60.** Children at play on the corner of Hester and Ludlow Streets.

pecially in autumn, when the sidewalks are filled with stalls set up by Chasidic Jews selling religious materials necessary for the High Holy Days. Here Essex Street probably has the city's highest concentration of shops selling religious articles as well as pious bookstores and strict kosher food shops. Intersecting with this part of Essex is Hester Street [59, 60]. To the east of Essex, Hester Street no longer exists, its former course now filled by the Seward Park Houses, a development put up in the 1930s. As mentioned, Hester Street was the predecessor to Orchard as the area's main artery of outdoor merchandising, the great street of the pushcart's heyday, recently commemorated as the very symbol of the old Jewish Lower East Side in the title of Joan Micklin Silver's film, *Hester Street*. Still, there are echoes of the old days along the part of Hester Street that remains to the west of Essex, even though one would never know from today's relative silence at the Ludlow Street corner [60] that it was the site of the "Pig Market" (page 5), the daily "shape-up" of the old garment industry, making it one of the noisiest and most crowded spots in this noisiest and most crowded of neighborhoods in New York.

THE OLD CENTER

The Jewish settlement of the Lower East Side began at this juncture of Essex Street, Canal Street and East Broadway, and the area has always been a center of Jewish life, although not always the primary one. At present it can well be considered the main center once again, since Jews both reside and do business in this district, unlike the stretches along East Houston, Orchard and Rivington Streets, which are solely business districts. But this Jewish center has become partly Chinese in recent years, as a vigorous and expanding Chinatown has encroached upon it from the west.

As one comes down to this intersection, today called Nathan Straus (formerly Rutgers) Square, along the east side of Essex Street, one first encounters William H. Seward Park [61], created by the demolition of two blocks of tenements in 1900 and named for Lincoln's Secretary of State. A bit of open space in an otherwise crowded area, it became an important recourse to sunlight and relaxation for residents of the surrounding blocks, and until quite recently it was a favorite domain for outdoor chess players. Now the elderly feel the park is too "rough" for such activities. Seward Park was a gathering place for crowds on election nights, during the heyday of *The Jewish Daily Forward*, across the street (its entrance can be seen in the rear of this picture, on the left). The Yiddish newspaper conveyed returns, often flashing them on a screen in front of the building. The park was considerably reduced in size during the 1930s, when the adjacent housing project that bears its name was built.

If any one institution acted as the heart for the bloodstream of the old Jewish Lower East Side, it was *The Jewish Daily Forward* [62, 63]. Founded in 1897, the *Forverts* (as it is called in Yiddish) was at first just one of several sectarian journals that had

been published on financial shoestrings by the socialist and radical groups of the Jewish immigrant community. But in 1903 Abraham Cahan, one of the founders of the paper, returned to it permanently as editor after two resignations in factional disputes and a four-year stint as an "American" journalist, working in the city room of the *New York Commercial Advertiser* under Lincoln Steffens. Schooled in modern American journalism in the era of Hearst and Pulitzer, Cahan knew how to popularize, and he did not hesitate to do so with the *Forward*, despite the complaints made by many of the old socialist intellectuals associated with the paper that he was degrading it. Introducing such celebrated features as *A Bintl Brief* ("A Bundle of Letters"), the Yiddish equivalent — with variations — of the lonely hearts column, Cahan won for his paper a following among the immigrants greater than had ever been dreamed of for Yiddish journalism: by the 1920s, the *Forward's* circulation of more than 200,000 was among the largest in the United States, for newspapers in any language. Under Cahan the *Forward* gradually abandoned the unyielding highbrow stance of old (although Cahan continued to publish the best in Yiddish literature alongside the articles of mass appeal) as well as the old rigid socialist ideology. By 1936 the newspaper, while never ceasing to call itself socialist, emerged as one of President Roosevelt's stoutest supporters.

Like the other papers — some of which had published out of the corners of printing offices — the *Forward* went through a succession of small offices in the few blocks surrounding Straus Square, until finally settling into the tenement at No. 175 East Broadway, and expanding into No. 173. In 1910, prosperity demanded that the *For-*

Left: 61. William H. Seward Park was created in 1900, when two blocks of tenements were demolished to bring some air and light into the Lower East Side. Below: 62. The old Forward Building, 175 East Broadway, is marked today by a sign in Chinese. While *The Jewish Daily Forward* operated in the structure, it was one of the most important focuses of the Jewish community. Opposite: 63. The entrance of the Forward Building.

Above, left: 64. After its inception in 1919, the Yiddish paper *Der Tog* moved into these converted townhouses at 185 and 187 East Broadway. Merged with another paper in 1950, it ceased publication entirely in 1972. **Above, right: 65.** The Garden Cafeteria, 165 East Broadway, still serves the dairy delicacies it did in its heyday, when Jewish intellectuals and journalists met there to join in heated discussions. **Left: 66.** The Educational Alliance was organized in 1889 to facilitate the assimilation of newly arrived immigrants. This building, at 197 East Broadway, was built for it in 1891.

ward seek temporary quarters nearby for two years while the old buildings were demolished and the present ten-story structure was erected in their place. For a long time thereafter, the *Forward* towered over its environs as *the* skyscraper of the Lower East Side, even though Jarmulowsky's Bank Building, a few blocks east on Canal Street (page 70) was taller. It was made even loftier by a huge neon sign on its roof which flashed the paper's name in two directions — toward the Manhattan Bridge in English and along East Broadway in Yiddish. Today, the building is occupied by a Chinese syndicate of developers. The *Forward*, still coming out six days a week, has moved to smaller quarters uptown, but the Chinese characters down the old building's western side remain uniquely balanced by the Yiddish letters that still proclaim the newspaper's name at the top of the facade.

Abraham Cahan, who lived until the age of 91 in 1951, remaining in control of the *Forward* to the last, made many enemies in the course of his Citizen Kane–like rise. Rival newspapers were formed — often by former members of Cahan's staff who had split with him — with this colossus as the most frequent point of reference by which to establish their own identities. Only the Communist newspaper, the *Freiheit* ("Freedom"), the bitterest of all of Cahan's foes, moved out of the neighborhood entirely, setting up its offices in Union Square. More typical was *Der Tog* ("The Day"), which, after its inception in 1919, took over the two converted townhouses at Nos. 185 and 187 East Broadway [64], only a few doors east of the Forward Building. They had been used for years by a preceding rival newspaper, the *Wahrheit* ("Truth"). Like the *Wahrheit* before it, the *Tog*, essentially liberal in outlook, never established a clear-cut political identity, but seemed determined only to maneuver around whatever position the *Forward* took. The result was that its columns presented a remarkably wide range of political opinions, ranging from conservative to what many called communist. What was more distinct about the *Tog* was its somewhat higher intellectual tone than that of the *Forward*, a quality which won it a solid readership among the well-educated. This tone veered over into a religious one beginning in 1950, when the paper merged with the *Morgen Zhurnal* ("Morning Journal"), an Orthodox religious paper of long standing. The *Tog–Morgen Zhurnal* ceased publication in 1972.

If the Cafe Royale was the principal hangout for people associated with the Yiddish theater, the writers for the Yiddish press usually congregated at the Garden Cafeteria [65], at the corner of East Broadway and Rutgers Street, just a few steps west of the Forward Building. A dairy restaurant like Ratner's, it specializes in blintzes, varnishkes and

67. Books in a multiplicity of languages are to be found in the collection of the Seward Park Branch of the New York Public Library, 192 East Broadway.

other non-meat dishes, but unlike Ratner's, it is a cafeteria. Indeed, it is one of the very last of those old cafeterias, once a New York institution, in which you collected a ticket at the door as you entered, which was duly punched for the appropriate prices by each food attendant as he served you. An American proletarian version of the European cafe, this type of cafeteria was the last remaining place in New York in which one could sit for hours over a cup of coffee and a piece of cake or a cup (or glass) of tea and piece of strudel. From East Broadway to the Broadway of the Upper West Side, they were favorite gathering places for Jewish intellectuals for about half a century. Until the adjacent Yiddish newspapers departed in the early 1970s, the Garden was still redolent with this atmosphere of heated political and literary discussions in Yiddish. Traces remain in the character of the food and service, in the general atmosphere and in the mural depicting the Jewish and labor history of the Lower East Side that fills one wall.

Just to the east of the Forward Building, on the far corner of Jefferson Street and East Broadway, is an institution that has been prominent in the life of the Lower East Side for almost ninety years, the Educational Alliance [66]. It was originally organized in 1889 as the Hebrew Institute by a group of associations representing the wealthier "uptown" Jews — most of them members of the German-

Jewish community that had itself once made the Lower East Side its principal neighborhood. As the settlement house movement was then under way, some of the uptown Jews recognized that they had a responsibility of their own to their poorer co-religionists downtown. Many were also eager to minimize a possible irritant to anti-Semites by helping Americanize the new immigrants as soon as possible. At the time when this building went up in 1891 (soon after which the name was changed), the focus on Americanization was so strong that none of its many classes, such as those in American history and government, were given in Yiddish. As a result, although the organization was intended primarily to give evening courses in adult education (as well as to serve as a settlement house with recreational facilities), the older generation stayed home, because of their poor or

Opposite: 68. St. Teresa's Roman Catholic Church was erected in 1841, when the neighborhood was still semi-rural. In 1863 it was purchased by the Catholic Archdiocese.

nonexistent English. After 1900 this situation was rectified, and the Educational Alliance gave courses in Yiddish as well. In recent years, Spanish has been added to the roster of languages.

Directly across East Broadway from the Educational Alliance is the Seward Park Branch of the New York Public Library [67]. Built in 1910, it houses sizable collections of books in Yiddish, Hebrew and Chinese, as well as those in English and other languages.

Back to the area west of the Forward Building, on Rutgers Street at the corner of Henry, is another still-flourishing institution descended from the pre-Jewish history of the area, St. Teresa's Roman Catholic Church [68]. The building was erected as the First Presbyterian Church of New York in 1841, when the neighborhood was still a semi-rural suburb. In 1863, when the neighborhood was becoming heavily Irish, it was purchased by the Catholic Archdiocese, and it has been a Catholic church ever since. It now serves the Hispanic and Chinese, as well as the English-speaking communities, and holds masses in all three languages.

EAST OF STRAUS SQUARE

Eastward from the old center, East Broadway and its immediate environs continue to show manifestations of their history as important streets of the New York Jewish quarter, although they are interspersed with the signs of more recently arrived ethnic groups as well, here principally Hispanic. For several blocks east of the Educational Alliance, the south side of East Broadway is an almost continuous chain of small Jewish religious establishments, headquarters of Chasidic rabbis, Talmud Torahs, yeshivas, and so on, but with an occasional Spanish church or business establishment in their midst. On the sidewalks of East Broadway [69, 70], one can readily see the presence of Orthodox Jews, both old and young. On the north side of the street, on the side wall of the Bialystoker Home for the Aged at No. 228 East Broadway, is a lively mural [71], depicting some of the history of the area, with special stress upon the needle trades, the labor movement and the Yiddish press.

At the point at which East Broadway ends in the intersection with Grand Street, is an ornate Classic Revival building that now houses a Ritualarium, or *mikveh* [72]. Built in 1904, the structure was for some years the home of the Arnold Toynbee Hall of the Lower East Side, an extension in the United States of the original London Settlement House movement that had inspired so many American versions. The initials "ATH" are still visible, carved in the stone balustrade over what had once been the main entrance. It is now replaced by windows, whereas two other entrances have since been built, one on either side of the old one. Even if the idea was originally an English import, the settlement house in general became one of the most American of institutions by the turn of the century, as vital a part of the im-

migrant neighborhoods in which they were located as were the churches and synagogues. For the children of the neighborhoods, the settlement houses, with their wide range of recreational and educational activities, shared honors with the schools as the central points of reference for everyday life.

The *mikveh*, or ritual bath, such as the building has now become, is an important part of life for Orthodox Jewish women, who must attend as part of the preparation for marriage, and who are required to cleanse themselves in it every month. Also noteworthy are the houses to the left of the mikveh in this picture, along the half-block of Grand Street leading to the Henry Street corner. These structures, some of them still showing their old dormered roofs intact, date back to the earliest years of the nineteenth century, when the blocks just south of East Broadway were a well-to-do Manhattan suburb.

Across the way from the mikveh, on the north side of Grand Street, are The Amalgamated Dwellings — also known as the Sidney Hillman Houses — an early experiment in cooperative housing, built in 1930 under the auspices of the Amalgamated Clothing Workers of America. Just to the left, a few steps north of Grand, at No. 7 Willett Street, is one of the outstanding sites on the Lower East Side, the Bialystoker Synagogue [73]. Built in 1862 as the Willett Street Methodist Episcopal

Opposite, top left: 69. A sidewalk discussion, East Broadway. **Opposite, top right: 70.** Electioneering, East Broadway. **Opposite, bottom: 71.** A mural on the wall of the Bialystoker Home for the Aged, 228 East Broadway, stresses the Jewish history of the area. The word in large Hebrew letters on the left, *Forverts,* is the masthead of *The Jewish Daily Forward.*

Opposite, top: 72. Today a *mikveh* (ritualarium) operates in the Classic Revival building that was erected in 1904 at the intersection of East Broadway and Grand Street as the Arnold Toynbee Hall of the Lower East Side. **Opposite, bottom: 73.** The Federal-style fieldstone Bialystoker Synagogue, 7 Willett Street, is a designated city landmark. It was built in 1826 to house a Methodist congregation. **Above: 74.** The Henry Street Settlement Playhouse, 466 Grand Street, was organized in 1915. The new Arts for Living Center, next to it, was one of the best examples of modern architecture on the Lower East Side. **Left: 75.** The entrance to the Henry Street Settlement Playhouse. The theater features many interesting new productions in drama and dance.

Left: 76. A Federal house, ca. 1830, is nestled between two tenements on Henry Street. **Below: 77.** Two Greek Revival town houses survive on Henry Street as reminders of more elegant days.

Church, the Federal-style fieldstone structure is a designated New York City landmark. The Congregation Anshei Bialystok ("People of Bialystok"), which had been organized on Orchard Street in 1878, bought this building in 1905. The ample congregation, made up of people living in the nearby housing developments, is still fully active. Because of its earlier history, this is one of the rare synagogues that do not face east. It also has the distinction of being New York's oldest building in which a synagogue is housed (as distinguished from the oldest one built as a synagogue — a distinction belonging to Anshei Slonim, page 33).

Adjacent to the synagogue, back on Grand Street, is the Henry Street Settlement Playhouse [74, 75], an offshoot of the celebrated settlement house described below. Organized in 1915 as a theater for the settlement's amateur productions, it soon became a house for professional theater as well. James Joyce's *Exiles* and S. Ansky's *The Dybbuk* both had their American premieres here, and it continues to serve as a stage for interesting new productions in drama and the dance. Graduates of the acting course given there include Gregory Peck, Tammy Grimes, Diane Keaton, Eli Wallach and Lorne Greene.

Henry Street, a block south of East Broadway, is today deteriorating in many places, even though it contains many fine surviving specimens of the New York Federal and Greek Revival town houses [76, 77], dating from the 1830s and 1840s. On the south side of the street, between Jackson and Montgomery Streets, surrounded by new housing, is one of the fine historic churches of New York, St. Augustine's Chapel [78]. Originally known as All Saints Church, it was built between 1827 and 1829 in the Federal style, of fieldstone used in much the same manner as that of the present Bialystoker Synagogue, which was erected during the same period. Like South Church in Boston, the building was equipped with a slave gallery into which the slaves were locked while their owners worshipped below. A melodramatic story is associated with this gallery and with "Boss" William Marcy Tweed, who was born nearby on Cherry Street. Tweed headed the infamous ring that drained the city's treasury in the 1860s and early 1870s. At the time of his mother's death, Tweed was a fugitive from justice, but nevertheless he attended her funeral at this church by hiding himself in the slave gallery. In 1881 the tower was topped by a cupola, which was recently removed. The name of the church was changed when it became a chapel of Trinity Church in 1949. Until the late 1960s, the place where it stands was the corner of Scammel Street, which was obliterated during construction of the adjacent housing development.

Further west along Henry Street at Nos. 263–267, are the original buildings and continuing headquarters of Henry Street Settlement [79], one of the most celebrated institutions of the Lower East Side. It is a monument to an American woman of true greatness, Lillian Wald. Born in Cincinnati, Ohio in 1867 to a German-Jewish family that had fled the old country after the failure of the 1848 revolutions, Lillian Wald was brought up in cultured and comfortable middle-class circumstances. At the age of twenty-one, suddenly feeling "the need of serious, definite work," she enrolled in the training school for nurses of the New York Hospital, and then entered the Woman's Medical College of the city in 1892. The following year, after accepting an invitation to organize home-nursing classes on the Lower East Side, she had a soul-searing experience with a sick immigrant woman in a shabby tenement house that caused her to leave medical school and devote her life to public health work in that neighborhood. She and a friend, Mary Brewster, lived at first in the College Settlement on Rivington Street, and then on the top floor of a tenement house on Jefferson Street, near the Educational Alliance. In a short time, Jacob H. Schiff, one of the wealthiest and most prominent of the uptown Jewish philanthropists associated with the Educational Alliance, became attracted to her work and obtained a permanent home for her at No. 265 Henry Street, a fine old Classic Revival town house that had been built, along with its neighbors, in 1832. There Miss Wald's "Nurse's Settlement" soon expanded its programs from public health to the full range of settlement-house work. Subsequently renamed Henry Street Settlement, it became as well known nationally as Hull House in Chicago, founded in 1889 by another great woman, Jane Addams (about whose work Lillian Wald had known nothing when she began her own). The two adjacent town houses, Nos. 267 and 263, were acquired by the Settlement in 1908 and 1934, respectively. Lillian Wald died in 1940, but the settlement she founded, which now has other branches in the neighborhood, carries on her work to this day.

Continuing west along Henry Street we come, at No. 203, upon what remains of Congregation Senier and Vilna [80], one of the outstanding small synagogues in the neighborhood. Constructed from a converted tenement house in 1893, the synagogue first housed the Congregation Makower of Poland. It was subsequently taken over by a group from Vilna, Lithuania, home of one of the great Jewish communities of Europe until Hitler destroyed it. The Senier congregation joined the Vilna congregation after the latter's synagogue burned in 1972. In 1975 this building was destroyed by fire, apparently the result of ar-

Opposite: 78. St. Augustine's Chapel was built on Henry Street, between Jackson and Montgomery Streets, in 1827–29. Designed in the Federal style, the interior contains a slave gallery. **Above: 79.** The Henry Street Settlement, 263–267 Henry Street, is one of the most celebrated institutions of the Lower East Side. Organized by Lillian Wald in 1893, the settlement has several branches in the neighborhood.

son. The gutted wreck now seems to stand as a symbol of what happened to its namesake, Vilna, itself.

The building that once housed the Rabbi Jacob Joseph School [81], at No. 165 Henry Street, is another shadow of its past self. Built in 1913 and named for the celebrated "Chief Rabbi" (pages 10 and 47), it was a full-time school of Jewish studies. Although it was run under Orthodox auspices, it also attracted the children of relatively non-religious families for many years. The playground next door to it was named in honor of Captain Jacob Joseph, a grandson of the Chief Rabbi, who was killed fighting with the Marines at Guadalcanal in World War II. In 1976 the school moved to premises on Staten Island.

On the other hand, the Etz Chaim Anshei Wolozin Synagogue [82], at No. 209 Madison Street a block to the south, still flourishes. A fine specimen of the many small synagogues that once filled the area, it was built in the early 1890s. Its circular window is now covered by boards and a Star of David, but otherwise its outward appearance remains intact and confident. Although only two blocks from the East Broadway center of Jewish settlement, its immediate setting is of a very different character, making it an admirable example of the effort to achieve real intercommunity living in New York.

Opposite: 80. At 203 Henry Street stand the burnt-out remains of the synagogue of Congregation Senier and Vilna. The building had been created by the renovation of two tenements. **Right, top: 81.** The Rabbi Jacob Joseph School was built in 1913 and named after the famous "Chief Rabbi." In 1976 the school moved to Staten Island. **Right, bottom: 82.** Built in the early 1890s at 209 Madison Street, the Etz Chaim Anshei Wolozin Synagogue still flourishes, even though the neighborhood in which it stands is now predominantly Hispanic.

WESTWARD FROM STRAUS SQUARE

West of the Forward Building, the Asiatic presence that has recently been moving in from Chinatown begins immediately to assert itself. There are Indians as well as Chinese, as can be seen in this view of the meeting point of Canal and Division Streets [83], taken looking westward from a point just a few steps west of Straus Square. The building at the corner of the intersection has merchants' signs aimed at Chinese and at Indian customers, respectively. This view, incidentally, depicts dramatically the geographical relationships of Lower Manhattan. At the end of the vista down Division Street (to the left), one can see beyond the ramp of the Manhattan Bridge to the towers of the municipal center, backed by the giant twin towers of the World Trade Center. To the right, along Canal Street, one looks past the high, ornate tower of Jarmulowsky's Bank Building to the low dome, in the distance, of The Manhattan Savings Bank at the corner of Canal and The Bowery, once the northeast corner of Chinatown.

Indians, a woman in a sari and a man wearing a Gandhi hat (or topi), are seen in a view of the intersection, looking northward from Canal up Ludlow Street [84]. The picture also shows what remains of the old Canal Street Theater, a movie palace built in the early 1920s. The auditorium of the theater, with its side exits and fire escapes, is visible on the Ludlow Street side, where part of the wall is covered by a mural, but the former front entrance on Canal (the third building from the left) now houses an electrical appliance store. (The former auditorium is now a warehouse.) The store, selling appliances wired for 220 volts for use in Israel, is one of several in this vicinity. There now also are a few such establishments catering to customers who want to send ap-

pliances to their relatives in India, or bring them as gifts during visits.

Opposite the old Canal Theater on Ludlow Street is a monument to another major institution of the old Jewish Lower East Side. The Kletzker Brotherly Aid Association [85], now disbanded, was what was called in Yiddish a landsmanshaft, one of many such societies of groups of immigrants, each of which came from the same hometown or area in Europe — in this case, Kletsk in Byelorussia. At its humblest, the landsmanshaft was simply an association of people from the old town who could provide the lonely immigrant with moral support, and perhaps with modest funds to take care of such stark necessities as medical care or burial. More prosperous associations could help struggling businessmen get started, or even build their own synagogues or gathering places, such as this one. Today one part of the building is used as a residence, the other as a funeral parlor.

One block farther west on Canal, at the Orchard Street corner, is the imposing facade of Jarmulowsky's Bank Building [86], seen in this picture

Opposite, top: 83. Looking west from the juncture of Canal and Division Streets, one is treated to a double vista — a comparative rarity in New York. To the left, terminating the view down Division Street, are the buildings of the Municipal Center and the twin towers of the World Trade Center. To the right, in the distance on Canal Street, is the dome of Manhattan Savings Bank. The tall building at the center of the picture is the former Jarmulowsky's Bank. **Opposite, bottom: 84.** There are several stores at the juncture of Canal and Division Streets which specialize in selling appliances intended for use in Israel and India. The fourth store from the left is housed in what was once the entrance to the Canal Street Theater, a movie palace built in the 1920s.

from the north along Orchard Street. Sender Jarmulowsky was a humble member of the earliest wave of immigrants who arrived from Poland in about 1870. It is said that he started out with a pushcart on Hester Street, but he rose quickly and had founded a bank for his fellow immigrants by 1873. By about 1895, Jarmulowsky was rich enough to put up this building, for years the tallest on the Lower East Side, even after the Forward Building went up fifteen years later. The institution's finances stood on shaky foundations, however, and the Panic of 1907, followed by the founder's death a few years later, made matters worse. The bank closed entirely during the First World War, and thousands of immigrant depositors, having placed much trust in a name that was one of their own, were ruined.

Just to the west and south of Jarmulowsky's, we come upon two more fine synagogues that are in danger. At No. 14 Eldridge Street, just south of Canal, is the Congregation Khal Adas Jeshurun-Anshei Lubz, better known as the Eldridge Street Synagogue [87]. It was erected in 1887 by the Congregation Khal Adas Jeshurun, which, having been formed by immigrants from Poland in 1856, is one of the oldest congregations founded by East European Jews in the United States, just as this synagogue is the oldest to have been erected by East European Jews. The facade, combining Romanesque, Gothic and Moorish elements, and dominated by a rose window in the manner of a cathedral, is unique among Jewish religious structures on the Lower East Side. The interior is equally splendid, for the firm that designed the building, Herter Brothers, specialized in interiors, having done drawing rooms for the mansions of Fifth Avenue. Although the building, housing a tiny congregation, may achieve landmark status and become a branch of the Jewish Museum specializing in synagogue objects, it is in perilous condition. Nearby, on Pike Street, is the congregation Sons of Israel Kalwarie [88], the other endangered synagogue. Built in 1903 by a congregation founded four years earlier, in its day it was the scene of some of the Lower East Side's most important religious occasions. Today it appears to have been abandoned entirely.

Left, top: 85. This building on Ludlow Street was built for the Kletzker Brotherly Aid Association, a *landsmanshaft* or organization devoted to helping newly arrived immigrants. **Left, bottom: 86.** For many years Jarmulowsky's Bank Building, at the corner of Canal and Orchard Streets, was one of the tallest structures on the Lower East Side. The bank, established by an immigrant of humble origins, collapsed during the First World War, ruining thousands of immigrant depositors. **Opposite: 87.** The splendid Eldridge Street Synagogue was erected in 1887. The facade combines Romanesque, Gothic and Moorish elements.

Above: 88. The Sons of Israel Kalwarie Synagogue on Pike Street has been abandoned entirely. Built in 1903, it was once the scene of some of the Lower East Side's most important religious occasions. **Opposite, top: 89.** A mural on Pike Street offers dramatic evidence of the recent expansion of Chinatown into the Lower East Side. **Opposite, bottom: 90.** St. Barbara Greek Orthodox Church, originally the Mishkan Israel Suwalki Synagogue, stands on Forsyth Street near the entrance to the Manhattan Bridge.

Pike Street seems to be one of the lines at which the old Jewish quarter most decisively comes to an end and is supplanted by Chinatown — note the Chinese commercial establishments alongside the Kalwarie Synagogue. The changeover was dramatized directly across the street from the synagogue by a large mural [89] depicting Chinatown. Today only echoes remain of the Jewish settlement that once existed beyond that line. At the bottom of Forsyth Street, near Division, facing one of the side walls of the entrance to the Manhattan Bridge, is St. Barbara Greek Orthodox Church [90], originally the Mishkan Israel Suwalki synagogue. The corner of Canal Street and The Bowery [91], was the original center of Yiddish theater before the First World War. Nothing of its old character is visible, owing to the demolition of buildings for the entrance to the Manhattan Bridge, which was widened after the Second World War.

The Chinese community has expanded into this sector all the way to the line formed by the Manhattan Bridge, and has even taken over some of the old surviving sites of Yankee Protestant days, just as the Jewish community had done, when at its height, in the Lower East Side neighborhoods. One example is the old Church of the Sea and Land [92] at the corner of Market and Henry Streets. This fine old Georgian-style structure, with Gothic Revival touches, was built as the Northeast Dutch Reformed Church in 1819 by a bequest of Colonel Henry Rutgers, a local landowner after whom Rutgers Street was named. Then known as the Market Street Church, it remained quite fashionable for about twenty years, but began to lose its luster as the neighborhood declined. In the 1860s it was taken over by the Presbyterian Church as a mission for sailors, receiving the name by which it was known for many years. It is now the First Chinese Presbyterian Church. This transformation has taken place at another old shrine for sailors, the Mariner's Temple [93], at the corner of Henry and Oliver Streets. The Greek Revival temple went up in 1843–44 as the third structure of the Oliver Street Baptist Church on the site. The ship's bell to the right of the entrance is a reminder of the days in the late nineteenth century when the church was a Baptist counterpart to the nearby Church of the Sea and Land. Today it houses a Chinese Baptist Congregation.

Only one block away from the Mariner's Temple is Chatham Square, the heart of bustling Chinatown, but also, in a quiet corner at the east side of St. James Place, the site of the Chatham Square Cemetery [94], the most ancient Jewish landmark in New York. Shearith Israel was the first Jewish congregation in the United States, having arrived in New York in 1654, during the governorship of Peter Stuyvesant. This burial

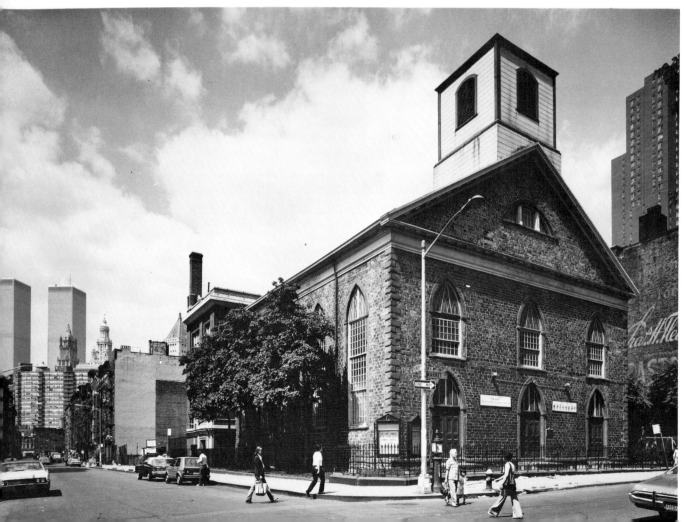

Opposite, top: 91. The corner of the Bowery and Canal Street was the center of Yiddish theater before the First World War. The imposing Manhattan Savings Bank used to mark the northeast border of Chinatown before the neighborhood expanded during the 60s and 70s. **Opposite, bottom: 92.** A fine Georgian-style structure with Gothic touches, the First Chinese Presbyterian Church was built in 1819 at the corner of Market and Henry Streets. For many years the church was known as the Church of the Sea and Land, a mission for sailors. **Above: 93.** The Mariner's Temple, at the corner of Henry and Oliver Streets, is another church with maritime associations that now houses a Chinese congregation. The handsome Greek Revival structure was built in 1843–44.

ground was acquired by the Congregation in 1682, the first (which has not survived) having been filled. It formed the physical focus for the Jewish community, for Shearith Israel — whose services were forced by English law to remain discreetly unnoticeable for years — did not erect a synagogue until 1729. (It was followed by a succession of buildings, culminating in the present Spanish and Portuguese Synagogue at 70th Street and Central Park West.) Interred in the cemetery are some of early New York's most distinguished Jewish citizens, most of them Sephardic, such as Mendes Seixas, who attended George Washington's first inauguration as a representative of the American-Jewish community. The cemetery was closed in 1831, and was succeeded by two others on Manhattan, both still extant: one on West 11th Street just east of Sixth Avenue; the other on West 21st Street west of Sixth Avenue.

94. The Chatham Square Cemetery is the oldest Jewish landmark in New York. Acquired in 1682 by Congregation Shearith Israel, it contains the remains of many of early New York's most distinguished Jewish citizens.

ON THE OUTSKIRTS

A full cup will brim over, and so did the life on the Jewish Lower East Side when it was at its height. There are several points just northwest of the geographical boundaries established in the Introduction (page 2) which are noteworthy.

The first is a reminder of a tragic event in the history of the Lower East Side — the Triangle Shirtwaist Company fire. At the corner of Greene Street and Washington Place, one block east of Washington Square, a plaque informs us that the Brown Building [95] of New York University once housed the Triangle Shirtwaist Company. By 1911, the garment industry of the Lower East Side had spread with the neighborhood's growth, ceasing to be a world of small sweatshops. Garment manufacturing was now done in factory spaces such as those occupied by the Triangle Company, which consisted of three lofts of 10,000 square feet each, on the top three floors of the ten-story structure, then known as the Asch Building. Completed in 1901 with wooden floors, trims and window frames, and with inadequate fire exits, the building was an easy mark for the disaster that struck it on Saturday, March 25, 1911, when the stories housing the Triangle Company burst into flames. Many of the trapped workers, almost all of them young women in their teens and twenties, the children of Jewish and Italian immigrants, tried to save themselves by leaping from the windows, and fell to their death on the street. By the time the fire was over, 146 were dead.

The shattering event gave rise to a historic response from the labor and reform movements in New York. As the plaque on the building — which today has a completely modern interior — says of the victims: "Out of their martyrdom came new concepts of social responsibility and labor legislation that have helped make American working conditions the finest in the world." One witness to the fire was Frances Perkins, who had been visiting friends in the neighborhood. She went on to have a career in social reform that culminated in her appointment by President Franklin Delano Roosevelt as Secretary of Labor.

Three blocks directly to the east of the Triangle fire site, on Lafayette Street just south of Astor Place, is the Public Theatre of the New York Shakespeare Festival [96], formerly the Astor Library and HIAS headquarters. The fur millionaire John Jacob Astor, whose mansion was located nearby, left a bequest upon his death in 1848 for building a library for public use on this part of his property. The south wing, built between 1849 and 1853, was designed by Alexander Saeltzer, a Jewish architect who also built the synagogue of Congregation Anshei Slonim (page 33). Astor's sons contributed to the building of the central and north sections; the entire Italianate structure was completed by 1881. For the next thirty years, the Astor Library was a resource for studious residents of the Lower East Side, among others. Beginning in 1912 the library's collection was amalgamated with the Lenox and Tilden collections and was installed in the newly built New York Public Library on Fifth Avenue and 42nd Street.

The building's subsequent history became even more involved in the Jewish life of the Lower East Side. In 1921, the structure was taken over by the United HIAS (Hebrew Immigrant Aid Society) Service. In the ensuing years, tens of thousands of Jewish immigrants were fed and sheltered there after they had passed through Ellis Island and before they entered the mainstream of American life. In 1965 HIAS moved uptown to larger quarters, and for a while the old building seemed

Opposite: 95. On March 11, 1911 the top three floors of the Brown Building (then called the Asch Building), was the scene of the tragic Triangle Shirtwaist Company fire. 146 people, most of them young girls from the Lower East Side, perished in the blaze. **Above: 96.** The building on Lafayette Place now owned by the Public Theatre of the New York Shakespeare Festival was opened in 1853 as the Astor Library. In 1921 the building was taken over by the United Hebrew Immigrant Aid Society, which helped ease many Jewish immigrants into the American mainstream.

threatened. But it was saved by the efforts of Joseph Papp, who secured it as a permanent home for the New York Shakespeare Festival and Public Theatre. After a clever renovation by Giorgio Cavaglieri, the building, which now houses several theaters of various sizes, opened to the public in 1967. The complex has become one of the most important theatrical institutions in the city. Several of its productions, most notably the hit musical *A Chorus Line*, have been moved uptown to Broadway after opening at the Public.

A few steps to the north and east of the Public Theatre is another institution which, like the Astor Library, belonged mainly to a world outside of the Lower East Side but was nevertheless an important part of its life. Cooper Union [97] was built between 1853 and 1859 by Peter Cooper, a true American jack-of-all-trades, who invented the "Tom Thumb" locomotive, aided in the development of the telegraph and the laying of the Atlantic cable and led a political career, flourishing as a businessman all the while. Cooper founded the school, a private institution dedicated mainly to art, architecture and engineering, as a tuition-free, nonsectarian, coeducational college, which it remains to this day.

The building (now called the Foundation Building to distinguish it from the school's newer structures) is architecturally one of the most distinctive in New York, among other things claiming to be the oldest building in the United States supported by rolled-steel structural beams. The brownstone and sandstone exterior is Italianate in a muscular, American-industrial style. In keeping with the philosophy of practicality that marks the whole building, the street floor was designed to accommodate stores, which remained there until recently. Although the building underwent a massive renovation in 1975, its basic character remains intact. The Great Hall, the celebrated auditorium below ground level where Abraham Lincoln spoke in 1860, was the site of many of the political meetings that were heavily attended by East Siders. It was here, for example, that Samuel Gompers made a speech to the shirtwaist makers' union during a general strike in 1909, only two years before the Triangle Fire. It was also a favorite spot for Lower East Side lecturers and debaters.

Opposite, top: 97. Built between 1853 and 1859, Cooper Union is one of New York's most distinguished landmarks. In its Great Hall Abraham Lincoln spoke in 1860 and many Lower East Side debates and lectures were held. Opposite, bottom: 98. An ornate molding over the bricked doorway is one of the few distinguishing marks left on the building that originated as Amberg's Theatre in 1888. After the First World War, as the Irving Place Theatre, it became a Yiddish theater, later a vaudeville and movie house.

Our last site is associated with the Yiddish theater, which showed a particular bent for spreading beyond the boundaries of the Lower East Side, at times even reaching Broadway. The former Irving Place Theatre [98], originally Amberg's Theatre, stands at the corner of Irving Place and East 15th Street. In the 1880s the neighborhood of 14th Street in the vicinity of Union Square was the heart of New York's theater district. The Academy of Music, which had been the city's principal opera house until the Metropolitan opened in 1883, was across the street at the east corner of 14th Street and Irving Place, a site now occupied by the Consolidated Edison headquarters building. Amberg's was built on the site of Irving Hall, a house for concerts, lectures and balls and a gathering place for a local faction of the Democratic Party. The building had been connected to the Academy of Music by an underground tunnel. Amberg's opened as a German-language theater December 1, 1888, when the 14th Street theater district was beginning to show the first signs of decline. But the area was finding new life as the northern boundary of the thriving German community, a trace of which still exists — Lüchow's Restaurant, which opened on 14th Street and Irving Place in 1882. Amberg's thrived until 1914, housing local companies as well as presenting stars from Germany, and providing "Dutchtown" with a place for lectures, concerts and public meetings. But the wave of anti-German feeling that swept the United States during the First World War led to the decline of Amberg's and, under different management as the Irving Place Theatre, it became a vaudeville and movie house. Then, in the spring of 1918, it was taken over by a Yiddish theater company whose co-owner and director was the rising young star from Russia, Maurice Schwartz, last in the line of great Yiddish tragedians. The company's first production, which opened September 10, 1918, was S. Ansky's *The Dybbuk*.

Owing to internal disputes, Schwartz broke with the Irving Place Theatre company two years later and formed a troupe of his own, which set itself up at the Garden Theater, now on Madison Avenue at 27th Street, and which became the Yiddish Art Theatre. As for the Irving Place Theatre, it went through several more incarnations, operating, among other things, as the Irving Burlesk in the 1930s, until burlesque was banned in the city. In the late 40s and early 50s it showed art films. Recently it was a truck warehouse for Klein's Department Store on Union Square, to which it is attached. At the moment of writing, the former Klein's is closed and in disuse, and so is the old theater. The masks of comedy and tragedy which still survive in the ornate molding over the doorway seem to be commenting on the history of the building itself.

BIBLIOGRAPHY

Hyman B. Grinstein, *The Rise of the Jewish Community of New York, 1654–1860*. Philadelphia: The Jewish Publication Society of America, 1945.

Hutchins Hapgood, *The Spirit of the Ghetto*. Cambridge, Mass.: The Belknap Press of the Harvard University Press, 1967. (Reprint of 1902 edition.)

Irving Howe, *World of Our Fathers*. New York: Harcourt Brace Jovanovich, 1976.

Ada Louise Huxtable, *Classic New York*. New York: Doubleday Anchor Books, 1964.

King's Handbook of New York. New York: Moses King, Inc., various years.

David S. Lifson, *The Yiddish Theatre in America*. New York: Thomas Yoseloff, 1965.

Bernard Postal and Lionel Koppman, *American Jewish Landmarks, Vol. I: The Northeast*. New York: Fleet Press Corporation, 1977.

Jacob A. Riis, *How the Other Half Lives*. New York, Dover Publications, 1971. (Reprint of 1901 edition).

Moses Rischin, *The Promised City: New York's Jews, 1870–1914*. New York: Corinth Books, 1964.

Ronald Sanders, *The Downtown Jews: Portraits of an Immigrant Generation*. New York: Signet Books, New American Library, 1977.

Allon Schoener, editor, *Portal to America: The Lower East Side, 1870–1925*. New York: Holt, Rinehart and Winston, 1967.

Gerard R. Wolfe, *New York: A Guide to the Metropolis*. New York: New York University Press, 1975.

Gerard R. Wolfe and Jo Renée Fine, *The Synagogues of New York's Lower East Side*. New York: Washington Mews Books, New York University Press, 1978.